D14Ũ3926

WHEN SANDY HIT

THE STORM THAT FOREVER CHANGED NEW JERSEY

Published by Pediment Publishing, a division of The Pediment Group, Inc. www.pediment.com Printed in Canada

Table of Contents

Foreword

It came in with a fury rarely seen, and left unimaginable heartbreak in its wake. New Jersey has seen its fair share of storms in its history, but Sandy — whether you call it a hurricane, superstorm or post-tropical cyclone — was clearly different.

It was the storm that climatologists and meteorologists always feared would target the most densely populated portion of the United States, and struggled to believe was unfolding before them as the forecast came into focus. It was the storm that the region was warned about for decades, but storm-hardened residents couldn't fathom becoming reality. Even as the storm bore down on the New Jersey coast on Oct. 29, 2012, when it made landfall near Atlantic City, it seemed like it couldn't possibly get worse. But the winds kept roaring louder, and the water kept rising. Sandy, clearly stated, was the storm that broke New Jersey.

Throughout the state, the evening of Oct. 29 was horrifying. As Sandy pushed inland, winds toppled more than 100,000 trees and arcing power lines and exploding transformers lit up the night sky as more than half the state lost power. Record seas tossed homes off their foundations like children's toys, and pounded them into piles of floating debris. A 10- to 15-foot wall of water surged inland, swallowing entire communities and washing away countless dreams and memories for thousands of residents.

As the sun rose, obscured by still skies, a new nightmare revealed itself. The damage was unprecedented — tens of billions of dollars, a number that could eclipse New Jersey's entire annual budget when all is said and done. More than three dozen were dead, entire shoreline communities were reduced to rubble, the state's transportation system was crippled and more than 2 million people were left without power, some of whom wouldn't see light for weeks. A return to normalcy suddenly seemed out of sight.

But as the shock of Sandy faded, New Jersey's drive to overcome soared. Volunteers flooded the state with supplies and manpower while emergency officials cleared debris and began rebuilding roads. Gasoline lines, at first hours long, slowly faded. Block by block, the lights came back on. Residents returned to devastated homes, wiped tears away and went to work pulling out drywall.

This book documents New Jersey's evolution during Sandy, showcasing work from the scores of The Star-Ledger employees, who themselves fought through floods, power outages and their own personal losses to remain on the job.

It tells the story of a state broken by Mother Nature's awesome fury. It tells the story of a state determined to rise again.

COMPARING HURRICANE SANDY TO OTHER STORMS

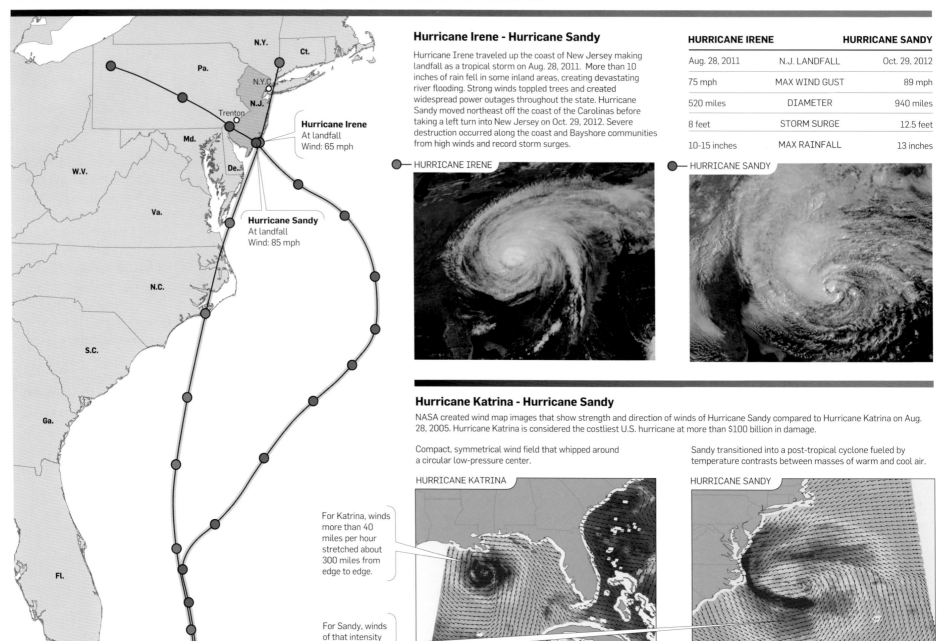

Hurricane Irene - Hurricane Sandy

Hurricane Irene traveled up the coast of New Jersey making landfall as a tropical storm on Aug. 28, 2011. More than 10 inches of rain fell in some inland areas, creating devastating river flooding. Strong winds toppled trees and created widespread power outages throughout the state. Hurricane Sandy moved northeast off the coast of the Carolinas before taking a left turn into New Jersey on Oct. 29, 2012. Severe destruction occurred along the coast and Bayshore communities from high winds and record storm surges.

HURRICANE IRENE		HURRICANE SANDY
Aug. 28, 2011	N.J. LANDFALL	Oct. 29, 2012
75 mph	MAX WIND GUST	89 mph
520 miles	DIAMETER	940 miles
8 feet	STORM SURGE	12.5 feet
10-15 inches	MAX RAINFALL	13 inches

HURRICANE IRENE

HURRICANE SANDY

Hurricane Katrina - Hurricane Sandy

NASA created wind map images that show strength and direction of winds of Hurricane Sandy compared to Hurricane Katrina on Aug. 28, 2005. Hurricane Katrina is considered the costliest U.S. hurricane at more than $100 billion in damage.

Compact, symmetrical wind field that whipped around a circular low-pressure center.

Sandy transitioned into a post-tropical cyclone fueled by temperature contrasts between masses of warm and cool air.

HURRICANE KATRINA

HURRICANE SANDY

For Katrina, winds more than 40 miles per hour stretched about 300 miles from edge to edge.

For Sandy, winds of that intensity spread out more than 900 miles.

WIND SPEED (MPH)   20   40   60

Map labels:

N.Y.
Ct.
Pa.
N.Y.C.
N.J.
Trenton

Hurricane Irene
At landfall
Wind: 65 mph

Hurricane Sandy
At landfall
Wind: 85 mph

Md.
W.V.
De.
Va.
N.C.
S.C.
Ga.
Fl.

100 MILES

Sources: NASA, NOAA   *Graphic by Andre Malok, The Star-Ledger*

Historic Storm

By Stephen Stirling, STAR-LEDGER STAFF

From early in its life, Hurricane Sandy seemed determined to write its own story.

That Sandy formed in the southern Caribbean was not unusual. Nor was it out of the ordinary for it to track north and hammer Jamaica, Haiti and the Bahamas. But what happened next landed Sandy in the meteorological history books.

No coastal storm or tropical system has ever made landfall in New Jersey traveling from east to west as Sandy did. A summertime storm system and a winter weather pattern fused to create New Jersey's storm-tossed autumn.

Generally, when tropical systems threaten the East Coast, their paths form a horizontal "U," curving toward and then away from the eastern coast of the United States as the storms follow a clockwise path around a semi-permanent high-pressure system in the Atlantic Ocean known as the Bermuda High – a common weather pattern during the summer months.

But Sandy came into an environment more reminiscent of January. A high-pressure system over Greenland acted as a stop sign for Sandy, trapping the storm and preventing it from taking the common track away from the coast. At the same time, a large upper-level low-pressure system carved a deep trough over the eastern United States, forcing the steering wind currents, known as the jet stream, to form a more northerly path up the East Coast.

As Sandy lurched north through the Bahamas, it seemed to have eyes on New Jersey from the very beginning. It paralleled the eastern coast, turning northeast to avoid North Carolina – typically a geographical protection the Garden State has against tropical systems.

Then it happened – the dreaded turn to the west.

Eventually, the blocking high gave Sandy nowhere to go and it gradually came under the influence of a cold front that had stalled over the Appalachians. The cold front acted as a magnet and pulled Sandy toward the coast, producing the unprecedented landfall near Atlantic City on Oct. 29.

In essence, Sandy did the opposite of what the past suggested, and it made its own history in the process.

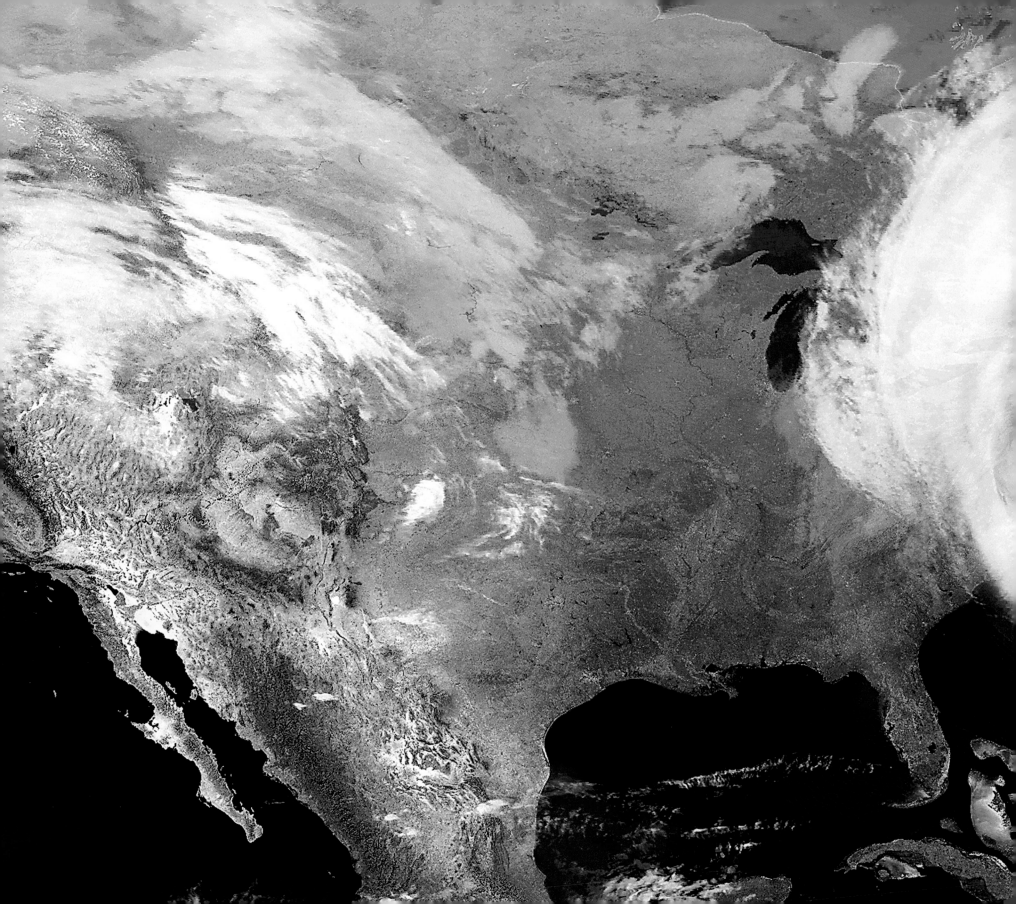

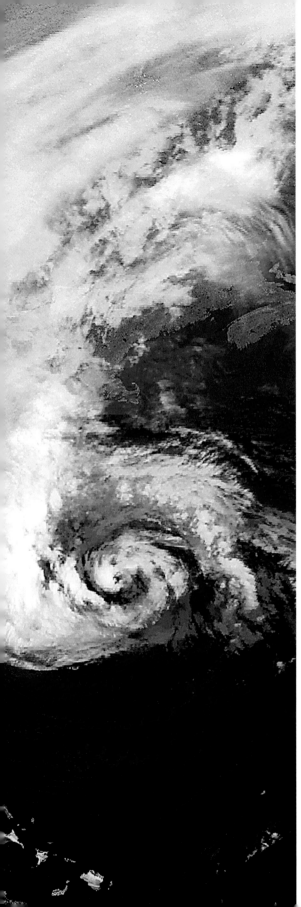

The Warning

ABOVE: Rich Medina, left, and Russ Bauer walk on the jetty at Barnegat Light as Hurricane Sandy makes its way toward Long Beach Island. JOHN MUNSON/THE STAR-LEDGER

LEFT: Hurricane Sandy churns off the East Coast on Oct. 28 in this satellite image provided by the National Oceanic and Atmospheric Administration. NASA PHOTO

RED-HOT GIANTS GRAB 2-0 LEAD

Bumgarner's 7 shutout innings keep Tigers in check as Series shifts to Detroit. In Sports

N.J. court OKs caps on school salaries

Superintendents sued over pay limits

By MaryAnn Spoto
STATEHOUSE BUREAU

In another win for the Christie administration in its battle to hold down school spending, a state appeals court panel yesterday said Education Commissioner Christopher Cerf has the right to impose salary caps on New Jersey's public school superintendents.

The ruling was the second legal blow this year to superintendents who claimed Gov. Chris Christie and Cerf unfairly targeted their salaries and other benefits they had accrued over their careers.

> "There is nothing arbitrary ... in the commissioner's effort to rein in spending."
>
> *Three-judge appellate panel*

State education officials said they were merely reining in wild spending by school districts that lavished their superintendents with pay and benefits not commensurate with their jobs.

In the 27-page appellate ruling, the three-judge panel said Cerf's plan to base superintendents' salaries on the number of students in their respective districts reflects the state Legislature's goal to tie their pay to per-student cost.

"The commissioner's action was consistent with that principle and there is nothing arbitrary, capricious or unreasonable in the commissioner's effort to rein in spending with salary caps based on enrollment," the decision said.

The New Jersey Association of School Administrators and three superintendents sued in January 2011 after the Department of Education adopted regulations setting up a pay scale that limited the salaries based on the size of their districts.

For example, those leading the smallest districts could be paid no more than $125,000, *SEE* **SALARIES,** *PAGE 8*

WHAT YOU NEED TO KNOW ABOUT PREPARATION, EVACUATION, YOUR POWER AND MORE. PAGE 4

The rise of Frankenstorm

Potential impact of monster weather combination 'borders on rare to unprecedented,' climatologist says

By Stephen Stirling
STAR-LEDGER STAFF

The crosshairs are zeroing in on New Jersey.

With each passing hour, the Garden State is under an increasing threat of taking a direct hit from a powerful — and perhaps unprecedented — hybrid storm government officials have dubbed a "Frankenstorm."

Hurricane Sandy, which had sustained winds of more than 105 mph last night, is churning north along the southeastern coast and is expected to become a crucial element in a mutating monster of a storm that could bring a nightmarish combination of severe weather to New Jersey from Sunday through Halloween.

Record-setting coastal flooding, major river and road flooding, and a prolonged period of winds gusting over hurricane-force strength are all possibilities, forecasters say, though the exact track

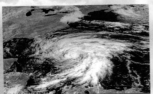

WORST-CASE SCENARIO: MUTATING INTO HYBRID STORM, SANDY WHIPS STATE WITH PROLONGED WINDS, RAIN AND RECORD FLOODING

of the storm continued to confound them last night.

"This is going to be one where we're going to be flying by the seat of our pants as meteorologists," said Steven DiMartino, owner of NY NJ PA Weather, part of the Storm Surge group. "It has all the facets of difficulty of forecasting for a hurricane. But it also has all facets of difficulty of forecasting a nor'easter. It's going to have to be watched by the hour as it evolves."

As Sandy moves north through the western Atlantic Ocean, it is being penned in by several weather disturbances to the north, east and west, slowing its movement and leaving it little place to go but slowly up the coast. As this occurs, a low-pressure system diving southeastward is expected to begin to interact with Sandy, pulling it toward the coast and transforming it into a hybrid between a tropical *SEE* **STORM,** *PAGE 5*

Jersey Legislature no friend of bosses who demand Facebook access

Senate OKs bill that would fine companies $1,000

By Matt Friedman
STATEHOUSE BUREAU

The days of employers forcing workers to grant them access to their Facebook accounts may be numbered.

The state Senate yesterday passed a bill (A2878) that would fine companies $1,000 if they request or demand access to workers' or potential employees' accounts on social networking websites such as Facebook, Twitter, LinkedIn and Pinterest.

Workers would also get the option to sue for money lost if they fail to get hired or lost their jobs or promotions because of the employer's prying. Companies that violate the law a second time would face a $2,500 fine. Only law enforcement agencies would be exempt.

"I have been reading more and more about how businesses and corporations, and schools as a matter of fact, are requiring your Facebook information," said Senate President Stephen Sweeney (D-Gloucester), a sponsor of the bipartisan measure. "They're not entitled to that. You're entitled to some privacy."

Maryland and Illinois both have recently enacted laws on the books that apply to employers.

"It is illegal to invade someone's house for personal properties and open another person's mail. So, what gives an employer the right to forcibly access such a broad scope of personal information against an applicant's will?" said another sponsor, state Sen. Diane Allen (R-Burlington).

The Senate also passed a bill (A2879) that would ban colleges and universities from requiring prospective and current students to turn over their usernames and passwords. The students could sue, but the bill does not include a fine against the colleges.

"Even if a claim against an employer is without merit and the employer *SEE* **FACEBOOK,** *PAGE 5*

votes, they have their critics.

Stefanie Riehl, assistant vice president for the New Jersey Business and Industry Association, said her organization does not oppose banning employers from requiring employees to give up their usernames and passwords. But she said the bill is too vague and should not allow employees to sue.

"Even if a claim against an employer is without merit and the employer *SEE* **FACEBOOK,** *PAGE 5*

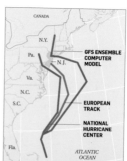

...H SCHOOL FOOTBALL
...EK 8 SCOREBOARD

	28	COLUMBIA	28	ORANGE	56	GLEN RIDGE	15	FOR MORE RESULTS, TURN TO PAGE 21
	20	NUTLEY	19	BELLEVILLE	21	EAST SIDE	12	

HURRICANE SANDY

■ **ARE YOU PREPARED?** *What you need to know before it hits, Page 9*

■ **FOR THE LATEST UPDATES ONLINE:** *Go to nj.com/sandy*

EYE OF THE STORM FOCUSED ON N.J.

ROBERT SCIARRINO/THE STAR-LEDGER
Gas station attendants are kept busy as residents wait to fill up yesterday at Costco Gasoline in Wharton.

State prepares for wind damage, power outages

By Stephen Stirling
STAR-LEDGER STAFF

There's no sugar-coating it — New Jersey should be bracing for potentially one of the worst storms in its history.

Forecasters and computer models continued to fine-tune the forecast for Hurricane Sandy yesterday, narrowing the window of possible landfalls from western Long Island to Cape May sometime late Monday night or early Tuesday. With Sandy expected to come ashore with the strength of a Category 1 hurricane, forecasters are warning of unprecedented coastal flooding, major river and flash flooding, and up to 48 hours of tropical storm-force winds or greater.

"This is a once-in-a-lifetime storm if these (conditions) materialize," said Tom Kines, a senior meteorologist at AccuWeather. "Even if it doesn't come ashore as a hurricane, I don't think people should let their guard down. The damage is going to be just as bad."

Officials and forecasters fear the storm, already blamed for at least 40 deaths in the Caribbean, could affect more than 60 million people as far west as Ohio, cause millions to lose power, record flooding and $1 billion in damages in New Jersey alone.

Low water levels could keep flooding in check

By Julia Terruso and David Giambusso
STAR-LEDGER STAFF

While New Jersey girds for what is expected to be a huge, possibly catastrophic storm, scientists and state officials say there may be a small silver lining for some residents: River and groundwater conditions are at or below normal levels, which could mean less inland flooding than during Tropical Storm Irene last year.

"All of the waters are a bit lower this year than last," said Larry Ragonese, a spokesman for the Department of Environmental Protection. "That will be beneficial for this storm because we're not overflowing the banks as we come into it."

August 2011 — when

Irene hit — was the sixth-wettest month on record. So when the storm dumped as much as 10 inches of rain in some areas, towns along the Raritan, Passaic, Rahway and Delaware rivers experienced intense flooding and extensive damage to homes and businesses.

But as this storm approaches, low to average river levels and forecasts of less heavy rain in north and central New Jersey mean residents of places such as Pine Brook, Fairfield, Little Falls, Wayne and Lincoln Park may avoid the semiannual nightmare of flooded streets, ruined furniture and a neighborhood exodus.

"The heaviest rain in this system has shifted from South Jersey down toward *SEE* **RIVERS,** *PAGE 7*

CONVERGING ON JERSEY

Forecast models differ on the path of the storm, but all predict a hit on the Garden State.

CANADA

N.Y.

Pa. — N.J.

Va.

N.C.

S.C.

Fla.

GFS ENSEMBLE COMPUTER MODEL

EUROPEAN TRACK

NATIONAL HURRICANE CENTER

ATLANTIC OCEAN

THE STAR-LEDGER
SEE **STORM,** *PAGE 6*

Star-Ledger staff memo

From Stephen Stirling, Star-Ledger weather reporter, to the staff on Sunday, Oct. 28

Synopsis

Sandy is expected to make landfall in New Jersey tomorrow night, somewhere along the Atlantic Coast, as a Category 1 hurricane. Rain should begin statewide as the afternoon progresses and winds will pick up as well. Tropical storm-force wind gusts are already occurring at the Shore. Conditions will deteriorate overnight and the entire state can expect to wake up to heavy rain and sustained winds of 35-45 miles per hour with higher gusts. Winds and rains will get heavier as the day progresses, peaking during the evening and overnight as the storm makes landfall. Conditions will gradually improve Tuesday afternoon.

Tides

Sandy is now likely to produce the worst tidal flooding New Jersey has ever seen. Minor tidal flooding is already occurring in some places and will only worsen as the storm approaches. The highest tides are expected to occur at 7-8 a.m and 7-8p.m. Monday.

In southern New Jersey and the Delaware Bay, the highest tides may occur tomorrow morning. In the north and Raritan Bay, they will likely occur during the evening high tide.

Along the Atlantic Coast, a 10-12-foot storm tide (storm surge plus astronomical tide) is expected to occur with waves of 10-15 feet breaking over it.

Essentially, take the water level now and add 10-12 feet vertically. Along the Raritan Bay, the storm tide could be 12-14 feet. This would cause catastrophic flooding of bayside communities and severe flooding in New York City, Hoboken, Jersey City and Newark.

This is an extremely dangerous situation. Storm surge kills more people in hurricanes than anything else.

If you are stationed on a barrier island, expect to be completely cut off from the mainland from Monday morning to Tuesday. Entire sections of the barrier islands could be submerged. Please find the highest ground possible before the storm worsens.

Anyone along the coast should identify safe locations and be constantly vigilant of rising waters. If you get stuck, emergency officials may not be able to rescue you during the height of the storm.

Heavy rains will exacerbate flooding along roadways away from the coast too, so be aware of your surroundings – your escape route could flood before you know it.

Winds

Winds will pick up overnight tonight and become sustained at tropical storm-force tomorrow. Power outages will begin to become widespread. As the storm approaches, all of New Jersey could experience hurricane-force winds. Along the coast, 100-mile-per-hour wind gusts are not out of the question.

The worst of the winds will occur in the evening Monday and overnight, but tropical storm-force winds could persist until Wednesday.

Driving will become dangerous as Monday progresses, if not impossible in some areas. Debris, such as tree limbs (or trees for that matter) will litter the streets and live power lines could be dancing all over the place. Street flooding will also be widespread.

If you are scheduled to leave the office anytime Monday night, getting a hotel room would be advisable.

Rain/inland flooding

Heavy rains should begin overnight, and could continue until Tuesday. As it does, flash flooding will likely begin occurring all over the state. Susceptible roads will become impassible. If we get more than six inches of rain (a distinct possibility now) major river flooding will begin occurring along smaller rivers. Larger rivers, like the Passaic, would not feel effects until later in the week.

Sorry if this all sounds pretty dire, but it is what it is. If you have any questions, feel free to ask. Stay Safe.

Preparation

ABOVE: Matt and Beth Starker stock up on D size batteries for flashlights and gas cans to fill to power the generator at their parents' home in Summit. Al Critelli, one of the owners of Summit Hardware, rings them up for the supplies in preparation for the weekend storm on Friday, Oct. 26, 2012. JENNIFER BROWN/THE STAR-LEDGER

LEFT: As Atlantic City prepares for Hurricane Sandy on Saturday, carpenters for Bally's Ed Goodwin, left, and Frank Jiacopello board up the doors on the boardwalk side of the casino. PATTI SAPONE/THE STAR-LEDGER

ABOVE: Ocean Avenue is closed at the south end of Belmar as officials have deployed two industrial pumps to drain Lake Como into the ocean as Hurricane Sandy makes its way up the coast. ANDREW MILLS/THE STAR-LEDGER

LEFT: Ron Skirkanish steps off his porch with a message for Hurricane Sandy posted on the front of his Manville home. Ron and his family have lived in Manville for 12 years. If this hurricane turns into trouble, it will be the fifth flood they have encountered. SAED HINDASH/THE STAR-LEDGER

THURSDAY, OCT. 25

- Hurricane Sandy, with sustained winds of more than 105 mph, churns north along the southeastern coast of the United States.
- The Garden State is under watch for record-setting coastal flooding, major river and road flooding, and a prolonged period of hurricane-force winds. Where, exactly, the storm ends up remains murky, but forecast models have slowly zeroed in on New Jersey, meteorologists say.
- The state Office of Emergency Management starts to review its assets and make sure the state is prepared.

RIGHT: A fisherman surveys the oceanfront at York Avenue in the south end of Spring Lake as Hurricane Sandy makes its way up the coast Oct. 26. ANDREW MILLS/THE STAR-LEDGER

- Sandy is listed as a Category 1 hurricane east of Florida and is blamed for at least 40 deaths in the Caribbean.
- Storm preparations in New Jersey ramp up. Schools warn of possible closures. Billboards are taken down near the Holland Tunnel, for fear hurricane-force winds would fell them. Voluntary evacuations are ordered in parts of Cape May.
- In an effort to mitigate flooding, levels at four northern New Jersey reservoirs are lowered and floodgates are opened at Lake Hopatcong and Pompton Lake.
- Forecasters warn of unprecedented coastal flooding, major river and flash flooding, and up to 48 hours of tropical storm-force winds or greater.
- The National Weather Service says the hurricane will likely be drawn back toward the coast by an approaching cold front, and explode into a monster storm that could cover the entire eastern third of the United States when it makes its expected landfall. A full moon Sunday night will keep astronomical tides at their highest, exacerbating any flooding that does occur.
- State Office of Emergency Management spokeswoman Mary Goepfert warns: "It's going to impact New Jersey. It's not going to skip us by, it's going to impact us in some way. Preparations really need to be done by Sunday afternoon."

ABOVE: Steve Savage of Jackson and Kathy Holleran of Monmouth Junction stock up on batteries at Home Depot in Monroe Township as they prepare for the arrival of Hurricane Sandy. Savage, who was hit hard from last year's storm Irene is also buying firewood and vinyl sheeting.

PATTI SAPONE/THE STAR-LEDGER

LEFT: A handful of boats remain in the water at High Bar Harbor Yacht Club in Barnegat Light 24 hours before the arrival of Hurricane Sandy to the to the Jersey Shore Oct. 27.

ANDREW MILLS/THE STAR-LEDGER

SATURDAY OCT. 27

- Sandy's impact is felt in North Carolina's Outer Banks, bringing rain and tropical-force winds. Forecasters warn the slow-moving storm could swamp coastal communities and dump as much as 8 inches of rain across the region, creating the additional threat of river flooding, before weakening Tuesday morning. Tropical-force winds are likely to reach well into Ohio.
- Hundreds of thousands of people around New Jersey pack up, gas up and stock up on supplies.

ABOVE: Regan Murphy, 6, helps her mom, Kelly Murphy, load supplies into the car at the Stop & Shop in Middletown on Saturday, Oct. 27. FRANCES MICKLOW/THE STAR-LEDGER

RIGHT: Night falls on Funtown Pier in Seaside Park 24 hours before the arrival of Hurricane Sandy to the Jersey Shore Oct. 27. ANDREW MILLS/THE STAR-LEDGER

ABOVE: The waves break only 30 yards from the St. Mary by-the-Sea retreat house on Sunday Oct. 28.

ARISTIDE ECONOMOPOULOS/THE STAR-LEDGER

RIGHT: Storm fencing already compromised at the Whiting Avenue beach in Manasquan, just north of Manasquan Inlet, Sunday morning as Sandy heads for the Jersey Shore.

ANDREW MILLS/THE STAR-LEDGER

Sunday Star-Ledger

$2.00 | OCTOBER 28, 2012

FINAL EDITION

NJ.COM

LOSS SHOWS RUTGERS HAS A LONG WAY TO GO

Politi: Why Kent State was a must win if Knights want respect. IN SPORTS

SAN FRANCISCO ONE VICTORY AWAY FROM WORLD SERIES TITLE

HURRICANE SANDY

- EXPERTS WARN: TREAT THIS STORM LIKE YOUR LIFE DEPENDS ON IT. **PAGE 10**
- EVERYTHING YOU NEED TO KNOW ABOUT STAYING SAFE, PROTECTING YOUR HOME. **PAGE 12**
- DESPITE ORDER TO EVACUATE ATLANTIC CITY, MANY PRESS THEIR LUCK AND STAY. **PAGE 14**

FACING NEW STORM, BUT NOT OVER THE LAST ONE

Residents devastated by Irene can't believe it's all happening again

By Amy Ellis Nutt / STAR-LEDGER STAFF

On Tuesday morning it will be 426 days between Irene and Sandy — 14 months between two, once-in-a-century storms.

In August of 2011, bridges collapsed, roads were swallowed by floodwaters and the belongings of thousands of New Jerseyans were saturated, shredded and carted away to community dumps.

As New Jerseyans once again prepare to withstand nature's assault, most can only shake their heads in disbelief. This just isn't supposed to happen, not two years in a row. With Hurricane Sandy churning toward the mid-Atlantic states and expected to make landfall in New Jersey on Monday night, The Star-Ledger wanted to know how a few of those who were devastated by Irene are coping with yet another "unprecedented" weather event.

JOHN GALLAGHER,
Jamesburg

John Gallagher remembers after Irene hit he spent three months of very long days repairing one of the two houses he owns. His home, at one end of Jamesburg, was spared, but not the home of his sister and brother-in-law, who moved in with him after the storm sent 2 feet of water gushing through their first floor.

PATTI SAPONE / THE STAR-LEDGER

SAED HINDASH/THE STAR-LEDGER

Top: Kristin Mueller, 23, of Manville sits in front of items removed from her family's home in August 2011 after Tropical Storm Irene. Above: On Friday, she prepares to remove her belongings as Sandy approaches. Below left: In Jamesburg, John Gallagher passes family photos found on the muddy floor to Clinton Miller as they help Ester Clanton, Gallagher's sister, clean up after Irene. Below right: (from left) Lisa Wagner and Jenn Fox document flood damage caused by Tropical Storm Irene at their store, Dash of Thyme in Denville.

NOAH K. MURRAY/THE STAR-LEDGER

JERRY McCREA/THE STAR-LEDGER

Jersey scurries as Sandy closes in

Residents gearing up to settle in or move out

By Mark Mueller
STAR-LEDGER STAFF

Heeding warnings that Hurricane Sandy could be The Big One, a mammoth storm with the potential to bring historic ruin to parts of New Jersey, hundreds of thousands of people yesterday packed up, gassed up and stocked up on supplies ahead of the onslaught.

Sandy's leading edge is expected to hit New Jersey this afternoon, strengthening as it merges with a cold weather system to the west.

Forecasters say the slow-moving storm could swamp coastal communities and dump as much as 8 inches of rain across the region, creating the additional threat of river flooding, before weakening Tuesday morning. Tropical-force winds are likely to reach well into Ohio.

Preparing for the worst, Gov. Chris Christie yesterday joined his counterparts across the Mid-Atlantic and Northeast in declaring a pre-emptive state of emergency. Most barrier islands south of Sandy Hook, including Atlantic City and its 12 casinos, were ordered evacuated by 4 p.m. today.

Christie, bluntly addressing the public during a televised news conference in Middletown, said Sandy needs to be taken seriously. The message seemed intended
SEE **STORM**, PAGE 13

TO OUR CUSTOMERS

The Star-Ledger will make every effort to print throughout Hurricane Sandy. Should conditions make that impossible, free digital access to our replica editions will be made available (see notice on Page 6) and NJ.com will continue to provide around-the-clock news and information from around the state.

GO TO NJ.COM/SANDY FOR UPDATES ON THE STORM

ABOVE: Pat Kearney walks by a store on the Washington Street Mall in Cape May on Sunday morning.
ARISTIDE ECONOMOPOULOS/THE STAR-LEDGER

BELOW: Tom Kowal, left, and Joe Rulli, owners of Joeys' Pizza and Pasta, board up their restaurant on Long Beach Boulevard in Beach Haven Crest as Hurricane Sandy bears down on Long Beach Island. They were prepared with their orange sign from previous storms. JOHN MUNSON/THE STAR-LEDGER

SATURDAY OCT. 27 (CONT.)

- Gov. Chris Christie declares a pre-emptive state of emergency.
- Most barrier islands south of Sandy Hook, including Atlantic City and its 12 casinos, are ordered evacuated by 4 p.m. Sunday.
- Shelters are scheduled to open in 18 of the state's 21 counties, with enough beds to accommodate 12,000 people. The Salvation Army, the Red Cross and food banks all have been placed on alert. The New Jersey National Guard is mobilized.
- The state's power companies arrange for out-of-state help to augment New Jersey crews and warn everyone that some outages could last as long as 10 days.

ABOVE: Kate Martinez of Seaside Heights lifts her dog Lucy over a fence on the boardwalk on Sunday, Oct. 28.
DAVID GARD/THE STAR-LEDGER

RIGHT: Storm watchers stroll on the boardwalk in Seaside Heights. DAVID GARD/THE STAR-LEDGER

ABOVE: Atlantic City residents wait in the lobby of the Atlantic City Convention Center before being evacuated to shelters on Sunday. NOAH K. MURRAY/THE STAR-LEDGER

OPPOSITE TOP: Gary Lowen of Beach Haven walks his dog past a shoe store as Hurricane Sandy makes its way toward Long Beach Island. He planned to leave LBI by Sunday's 4 p.m. evacuation deadline. JOHN MUNSON/THE STAR-LEDGER

OPPOSITE BOTTOM: Traffic is seen westbound over the Route 37 bridge between Toms River and Seaside Heights on Sunday. DAVID GARD/THE STAR-LEDGER

SUNDAY, OCT. 28 — WORST-CASE SCENARIO

- The storm is moving at 14 mph and is about 470 miles south of New York City, but the rain and surf start to pummel New Jersey.
- All public transportation in New Jersey is suspended. New York City shuts down the subway.
- Thousands of Atlantic City residents walk to the Atlantic City Convention Center for evacuation.
- Despite an evacuation order, some Long Beach Island residents decide to board up, batten down and stay put. In Seaside Heights, members of the fire department go door to door trying to chase the last few stragglers from their homes.

LEFT: Steven Bernatowicz, 52, of Toms River hunts for treasure under a section of the boardwalk that had been removed for renovation as Hurricane Sandy approaches Seaside Heights on Sunday evening. DAVID GARD/THE STAR-LEDGER

The Star-Ledger

$1.00 | **MONDAY, OCTOBER 29, 2012**   **FINAL EDITION**

NJ.COM

SAN FRANCISCO SWEEPS DETROIT. IN SPORTS

— HURRICANE SANDY —

- ■ Already flooded, many shore towns scramble to evacuate. Page 8
- ■ Where the storm will make landfall and what's closed today. Page 5
- ■ Live help at nj.com. Our reporters answer your questions around the clock.

State forecast: A catastrophe

A satellite image shows Hurricane Sandy bearing down on the East Coast, especially New Jersey. The combination hurricane-nor'easter is expected to bring record storm surges.

NATIONAL OCEANIC AND ATMOSPHERIC ADMINISTRATION

Faith that house built on sand will remain foundation of rock

Mark Di Ionno
nj.com/diionno

Just before the rains came and the winds picked up, Sister Mary Ann Mulzet was walking the dark, empty halls of the St. Mary by-the-Sea

plywood over windows at some of Cape May's most venerable — and vulnerable — old hotels, like the Congress, where Abe Lincoln once stayed, the order

TO OUR CUSTOMERS
The Star-Ledger will make every effort to print throughout Hurricane Sandy. Should conditions make that impossible, free digital access to our rep

N.J. BATTENS DOWN, BRACES FOR DEVASTATING FLOODING

By Amy Ellis Nutt and Stephen Stirling
STAR-LEDGER STAFF

With a megastorm knocking on New Jersey's door this morning, the state braced for a meteorological monster that experts struggled to find adjectives to describe.

"It's basically the worst-case scenario coming true," said Gary Szatkowski, meteorologist in charge at the National Weather Service's Mount Holly office. "It will be beyond anything anyone has ever experienced."

ABOVE: Longtime residents Bill and Donna Kaiser and their dog, Molly, in their home on 19th Street in Belmar as northeast winds from the outer bands of Hurricane Sandy begin to batter the Jersey Shore. The Kaisers moved all of their belongings out of their basement in anticipation of the ocean washing into their home. ANDREW MILLS/THE STAR-LEDGER

TOP: Carla Sinski of Cedar Grove looks at the surf after securing her boat at a nearby marina as the storm makes its way toward Long Beach Island. JOHN MUNSON/THE STAR-LEDGER

RIGHT: A couple and their dog cross a street as Sandy nears Seaside Heights on Sunday evening. DAVID GARD/THE STAR-LEDGER

CHAPTER THREE

The Storm

ABOVE: An NJ Transit police officer monitors Hurricane Sandy in the Support Room of the State Police Regional Operations Intelligence Center in Ewing on Monday, Oct. 29. TONY KURDZUK/THE STAR-LEDGER

LEFT: Waves from Hurricane Sandy pound the Seaside Heights Boardwalk on Monday, Oct. 29.

DAVID GARD/THE STAR-LEDGER

48 HOURS THAT FOREVER CHANGED NEW JERSEY

By Amy Ellis Nutt, STAR-LEDGER STAFF

Sandy's devastation was widespread, but perhaps it resonated most along the Jersey Shore, where seemingly every family has made memories, where every kid has played Skee-Ball in a boardwalk arcade and where the sausage-and-peppers sandwiches tasted unlike anything we ever put in our mouths. This morning, there are only splinters where towns stood and there is a roller coaster in the Atlantic. The owners vow to rebuild, the residents to return. The resolve is the same everywhere you go, even as people struggle to understand what happened last week.

With that in mind, this is the blow-by-blow account of Sandy's deadly path into New Jersey. It was based on eyewitness accounts from Shore residents and officials, including many who rode out the storm on the barrier islands. Also included are meteorological data and interviews with officials who describe how the storm stalked the state for days before turning on New Jersey and unleashing a double-fisted fury beyond all imagining.

Ancient mariners believed the tides were the angry breathing of a sea creature chained to the ocean floor.

In Cape May on Sunday morning, Oct. 28, with Hurricane Sandy still 300 miles from shore, the tides, instead, beckon surfers, riding wind-driven swells off the Ocean Street beach.

Just inland, residents and business owners take the usual precautions against an impending storm. At the Congress Hall, where Abraham Lincoln once stayed, workers nail plywood over the ground-floor windows and doors.

Down Perry Street at the Bayberry Inn, a

ABOVE: No beach remains uncovered by seawater in Seaside Heights.
DAVID GARD/THE STAR-LEDGER

RIGHT: Edward Febus, 44, makes his way back to his house as Hurricane Sandy approaches Seaside Heights on Monday, Oct. 29. He had evacuated his wife and daughter and was planning to join them, but his car would not start, leaving him no escape from the storm and no choice but to ride it out. DAVID GARD/THE STAR-LEDGER

ABOVE: Waves crash on the amusement pier in Atlantic City as Hurricane Sandy hits.

NOAH K. MURRAY/THE STAR-LEDGER

LEFT: A Lavallette police officer watches as Hurricane Sandy pushes the surf over the dunes and onto Harding Ave. at high tide in Ortley Beach on Monday, Oct. 29. DAVID GARD/THE STAR-LEDGER

BELOW: A man crouches to get a better angle while taking a photograph of the storm surge during morning high tide. ARISTIDE ECONOMOPOULOS/THE STAR-LEDGER

ABOVE AND RIGHT: The storm surge during morning high tide comes over the dunes onto Beach Avenue in Cape May on Monday, Oct. 29.

ARISTIDE ECONOMOPOULOS/THE STAR-LEDGER

OPPOSITE: Joseph Guerriero looks at the Atlantic Ocean as Hurricane Sandy makes its way toward the Ortley Beach section of Toms River.

JOHN MUNSON/THE STAR-LEDGER

Boyd studies the forecast on the computer in his office, zeroing in on the radar predicting the storm's path.

"Follow the map, follow the map," he repeats to himself.

At this moment, with Sandy still only a swirl of color on a meteorologist's computer screen, few up and down New Jersey's 127-mile-long Shore could mistake the Atlantic for a monster.

Twenty-four-hours later, they will.

Although meteorologists record the first tropical storm-force winds in Cape May at 7 a.m. Sunday, by early afternoon, with Sandy still moving slowly north, there remains a slim possibility it still might skirt New Jersey and turn eastward. That's what Chief Boyd is counting on. But that door out to the east, away from land, is rapidly closing.

COME THE RAINS

At exactly 12:37 p.m., according to meteorological reports, the storm's first rain falls on Cape May Point. Outside the volunteer fire department, Joe Nietubicz takes down the American flag. The department's 16-foot flat johnboat and Carolina skiff are hauled out and readied, while a crew preps the fire engines to be moved to higher ground.

On Sunday evening, as more coastal residents seek inland shelter, the hotels and motels along state Highways 35, 36 and 9 flash red "No Vacancy" signs. Wind and rain continue to whip the ocean. Even the inlets and marshes seethe with surly whitecaps.

Most people on the barrier islands take the evacuation orders seriously as experts track Sandy's massive 1,000-mile-wide arms swirling and churning just off the Carolinas. What they are also watching is a stubborn, low-pressure system hugging the Appalachians, pulling Sandy to the west. It's a game of tug of war, and by 2 a.m. Monday, with wind gusts reaching 60 mph

Victorian bed-and-breakfast, owners Andy and Toby Fontaine shuffle the patio furniture inside.

"We're staying, basically, because I can't think of any place to go," Andy Fontaine says.

The forecast has hovered like a sword of Damocles over the state for days. Plenty of time to get ready — shore up windows, move possessions to second floors, purchase batteries and water. That's what New Jersey did last year, right before Irene hit. But this is different — a hurricane buddying with a nor'easter. Almost everyone believes the damage will be substantial and the pain, perhaps unprecedented. But few are prepared for the meteorological time bomb set to explode over New Jersey's coast, or the suddenness of a tidal surge that in the time it takes to watch a movie, will forever change the geography of the state.

While the Fontaines prepare for the storm, at Cape May Point Sister Mary Ann Mulzet moves briskly along the empty halls of St. Mary by-the-Sea, a massive Victorian structure built more than 120 years ago as a resort hotel. For the past 100 years, however, the Sisters of St. Joseph have called the 130-room hotel their retreat house. It stands sentinel on the southernmost piece of land in New Jersey — the last spit of earth where the toe of the Garden State meets the Atlantic.

From the windows of this Tuscan red-roofed retreat, an observer can take double delight in watching the sun rise and set.

By 11:30 a.m., Sister Mary has checked all the windows and heads for the convent house in Wildwood, where she will join her fellow sisters in evacuating before the storm.

"We're relying on the prayers of all the sisters who made retreats here," Sister Mary says, as sirens whine in the background. "We believe the power of prayer will keep it safe."

In Seaside Heights, police Chief Thomas J.

ABOVE: Jared Butler of Spring Lake Heights walks out onto the beach at the Belmar Fishing Club pier Monday morning as it is pounded by relentless waves. "I couldn't get any closer," he said. "The storm is too intense." ANDREW MILLS/THE STAR-LEDGER

RIGHT: George Gilmore of Seaside Heights takes pictures of the Atlantic Ocean from the Surf Club on Ocean Ave. as Hurricane Sandy makes its way toward the Ortley Beach section of Toms River. JOHN MUNSON/THE STAR-LEDGER

FAR RIGHT: Justin Distler and his sister, Caitlin Distler of Middletown, check out Sandy at Sea Bright during Hurricane Sandy in Sea Bright on Monday, **Oct. 29.** ED MURRAY/THE STAR-LEDGER

LEFT: Staples in Milltown posts a sign on the front door: "SOLD OUT of C-cell batteries (and) D-cell batteries." Most if not all stores in the area were sold out of those items as residents prepared for Hurricane Sandy. PATTI SAPONE/THE STAR-LEDGER

FAR LEFT: Lisa Little from Carneys Point struggles with her umbrella as Hurricane Sandy hits New Jersey. JOHN O'BOYLE/THE STAR-LEDGER

BELOW: John Dahl tries to fix his stalled engine as Hurricane Sandy makes its way toward Point Pleasant Beach. JOHN MUNSON/THE STAR-LEDGER

ABOVE: A front loader pushes sand and debris back toward the ocean on Harding Avenue in Ortley Beach after Hurricane Sandy pushed waves over the dunes Monday, Oct. 29. DAVID GARD/THE STAR-LEDGER

inland and a high tide washing water over miles of dunes, that door to the east — New Jersey's only escape hatch — slams shut.

When Chief Boyd sees the hurricane make an abrupt left-hand turn on the computer screen, he says to himself, "We're screwed." Immediately he begins calling in more officers and making arrangements to pull cruisers off the island — cars will be useless, and worse, one-ton missiles in a flood.

The unthinkable is now the inevitable. A storm of historic proportions and intensity is rushing headlong toward one of the most densely populated coastlines in the world. Sixty-five million Americans, 9 million of them in New Jersey, are in her path. And those remaining on the barrier islands are in the bull's-eye.

Chief Boyd wakes up Monday morning at police headquarters, where he has spent the night. By 8 a.m. his phone is ringing nonstop. Boyd has lived nearly his entire 51 years on the island. In 1991, married and with three young children, he moved inland, to Toms River. Sitting at his desk, he takes one call after another from Seaside Heights residents who have evacuated. They've

TOP: Pumps atop a levee at the end of Floodgate Road in Greenwich Township, Gloucester County, as Hurricane Sandy hits New Jersey. The levee sits at the end of the lowest part of the county, which means that it must absorb most of the region's rainwater. The levee opens to allow the tributary to get rid of the excess rainwater, but if the Delaware River climbs above the wall, it will be rendered useless. JOHN O'BOYLE/THE STAR-LEDGER

BOTTOM: Members of the New Jersey National Guard monitor Hurricane Sandy in the Support Room of the State Police Regional Operations Intelligence Center in Ewing.
TONY KURDZUK/THE STAR-LEDGER

seen or heard the forecast by now, and they want to come back for their possessions. Boyd will have none of it. No, he tells them. The bridges are closed, the evacuation mandatory.

Outside, it is gray, humid and chilly. Gusting winds and driving rain challenge the balancing skills of pedestrians. In nearby Lavallette, Jim McCann watches the first high tide surge split the dunes and wash down the street. The water is no more than ankle-deep, but it's fast-moving and in a matter of minutes swallows the dune at the end of the block. Water spews across the boardwalk

and spits upward between the planks.

At Joey Harrison's Surf Club in Ortley Beach, the surge rushes through windows and doors. Furniture, freezers — anything not bolted down — is swept out, but the building remains intact. Not so a nearby outdoor restaurant, which crumples and shreds.

As Sandy stalks the coast, thundering northward, Karen Ludwig, in Raritan Bay, decides she's not taking any chances. She's lived in Union Beach, on a street that runs up against the bay, for 52 years and she's fled every storm since the Ash

Wednesday nor'easter of 1962.

"There was Donna, or maybe Gloria," Ludwig says. "(Then) Floyd ... Oh, and Irene. We left last year for Irene."

Ludwig and her husband, Richard Kuti, decide

ABOVE: An airport employee arrives for work where sandbags were installed in many places for protection of water intrusion during Hurricane Sandy at Newark Liberty Airport.

JERRY MCCREA/THE STAR-LEDGER

to check into the Best Western in Hazlet.

At the police station in Seaside Heights, Boyd gets up from his desk. The silver-haired chief leans on a cane. Three weeks ago, he underwent knee replacement surgery. He meets with Seaside Heights Mayor Bill Akers to make final preparations, and by noon hits the road in his police truck with an officer, driving up and down Ocean Boulevard, keeping an eye on the boardwalk and Casino Pier.

He wants to get a good look at the ocean, so Boyd directs the officer to drive up onto the sea-swept boardwalk. When a huge wave flies over the railing and rushes under the truck, it lifts it for a moment, rocking it back and forth. For the first time, Boyd is genuinely frightened about the coming storm.

TOP LEFT: This man was disappointed to be needing accommodations at a makeshift airport shelter during Hurricane Sandy at Newark Liberty Airport. JERRY MCCREA/THE STAR-LEDGER

TOP RIGHT: Flights to Toronto were among the many canceled during and after the storm. JERRY MCCREA/THE STAR-LEDGER

BOTTOM: Carlos Ferreira of Portugal shares a fast-food pizza with his daughter, Ana, in a makeshift shelter for stranded travelers. JERRY MCCREA/THE STAR-LEDGER

ABOVE: People come out to the Jersey City waterfront where the water levels of the Hudson River reached the seawall due to Hurricane Sandy. JENNIFER BROWN/THE STAR-LEDGER

OPPOSITE LEFT: Hurricane Sandy hits Atlantic City area. NOAH K. MURRAY/THE STAR-LEDGER

OPPOSITE RIGHT TOP: At the Jersey City waterfront, an employee of Waterware, which was hired by the Jersey City Municipal Utilities Authority, pumps water out of the sewer system to help prevent flooding. JENNIFER BROWN/THE STAR-LEDGER

OPPOSITE RIGHT BOTTOM: A road sign on Route 10 in Morris Plains tells the story as Hurricane Sandy churns its way through New Jersey and the Northeast. TIM FARRELL/THE STAR-LEDGER

ABOVE: Port Authority police turn drivers away from the Holland Tunnel, closed because of Hurricane Sandy. JENNIFER BROWN/THE STAR-LEDGER

RIGHT: Pedestrians walk past a Main Street building during Hurricane Sandy in Bound Brook on Monday, Oct. 29. ED MURRAY/THE STAR-LEDGER

ABOVE: A tree fell shearing a porch off one house and heavily damaging another during Hurricane Sandy on Birks Place in Newark. JERRY MCCREA/THE STAR-LEDGER

OPPOSITE: A tree crushed this house on the corner of Pine and Dewey avenues in Manasquan. Borough police were able to remove all residents with no major injuries, but the house was in danger of collapse. ANDREW MILLS/THE STAR-LEDGER

By 3 p.m. Monday, Sandy's cloud cover reaches as far north as Canada and as far west as Iowa. The low pressure from the west and a high pressure system from the Northeast fence the storm in over the Mid-Atlantic. Alarmingly, even at low tide along the New Jersey coast the water remains abnormally high — for a high tide, that is. Like stacking Mount McKinley atop Mount Kilimanjaro, Monday's two high tides will essentially form an enormous column of water, poised to deliver misery and mayhem to millions.

Boyd spends the afternoon trying to convince residents who have remained behind, to leave. When they refuse, he can only shake his head in disbelief.

"They think they're gonna be able to sit there and stop Mother Nature from pouring millions of gallons of water down the street? To save their house?!"

Anyone who doesn't have a second floor or attic to retreat to, Boyd orders out of town.

Around 3 p.m., on the bridge between Toms River and Seaside Heights, Toms River police Chief Michael Mastronardy swerves violently, hitting his brakes, to avoid being creamed by several utility poles that crash thunderously to the ground, a mere hundred feet in front of him. Shaken, he calls Boyd.

"Tommy," Mastronady says, trying to laugh. "I

almost got crushed by telephone poles."

The most important route between the island and mainland is now impassable.

A full moon officially arrives a bit before 4 p.m., helping to turn Sandy's high tide surge into a tsunami-like wave of floodwater up and down the East Coast. In New York harbor, instruments will later record a peak wave of 32 feet.

What's coming, no one, not even Boyd or his officers, can foresee — a calamitous rush of water is about spring on the Shore. For two terrifying hours it will spin and punch its way inland.

The power is out all along the coast by 7 p.m. and swells from both the bay and ocean begin to pool in some sections of Seaside Heights. Heavy flooding in Ortley Beach and Lavallette has made Mantoloking Bridge inaccessible. The barrier island is now entirely cut off.

Fewer than 20 miles from the coast, Sandy weakens slightly and the National Hurricane Center says it is now a nor'easter with 85 mph winds. The classification is meaningless for residents of New Jersey's barrier island. When Sandy makes landfall around 8 p.m., it smacks the state at hurricane strength.

BRAVING THE STORM

Boyd is in his truck with Fire Chief James Samarelli, who is at the wheel. They turn right onto Sampson Avenue and are nearly hit by a wooden lifeguard boat slicing through the floodwater. A wall of water is headed directly for them, bringing a second lifeguard boat. Samarelli jerks the truck to the right. A large piece of the boardwalk, ripped away by the waves, slams into the front of the flatbed truck. Boyd looks down at his suddenly cold feet. Seawater is rushing into the cab and a 6-foot-tall swell lifts the truck and begins pushing it sideways, into a telephone pole.

Boyd knows if they get pinned and flip, they'll drown. He thinks about how he and the other officers are out here just trying to save people's lives.

ABOVE LEFT: Mike Shumacker takes a look at the surf before Hurricane Sandy arrives in Atlantic City. NOAH K. MURRAY/THE STAR-LEDGER

ABOVE RIGHT: Wipers clear a line of sight for a driver in Seaside Heights. DAVID GARD/THE STAR-LEDGER

RIGHT: A section of boardwalk in Atlantic City destroyed by storm. NOAH K. MURRAY/THE STAR-LEDGER

OPPOSITE: A wall of sea foam rushes down the boardwalk as Hurricane Sandy strikes Seaside Heights on Monday evening, Oct. 29. DAVID GARD/THE STAR-LEDGER

Instead, it looks like he's going to die. Another swell hits the windshield. Samarelli desperately throws the car into reverse trying to back up and get traction. Another wave, and the truck is sent swirling down Sampson Avenue. The piece of boardwalk that was clinging to the grill of the truck shakes loose. Somehow Samarelli maneuvers the truck onto firmer ground.

"Time to go to headquarters," Boyd says.

Waves 10, 20 feet high pound up, over and through the dunes and rush with marauding intensity down streets and across boulevards violently wrapping around motels, ice cream parlors and cozy breakfast nooks. Houses are ripped from foundations, cars tumble like bathtub toys and boats become ghost ships sailing through flooded, amputated towns.

When the water reaches 13.3 feet above normal, Sandy Hook tidal station breaks its all time record by more than 3 feet — then washes away, the water still rising.

A man in Seaside Heights grips a low-hanging tree branch, clinging on to it for dear life, as water rises to his chest.

"Please save me!" he calls to Boyd. "Please save me! I'm scared for my life!"

Boyd and Samarelli grab the man and drag him through the water to the truck.

All over Seaside, Boyd and his 18 officers scoop up residents from attics, roofs and trees and deliver them to dry land. If it's possible, the storm seems to be even more treacherous. The chief decides it's too dangerous to be out and pulls his team back into the station. By Boyd's count, they've saved 36 lives.

Jack Buzzi from Normandy Beach in Toms River is talking on the phone with a neighbor who lives across the street. It's about 9 p.m., an hour since the high-tide surge, and the water has chased the woman to her second floor. Buzzi can also see out his window that she's stranded. The next moment a wave blasts the woman's house off its foundation, shattering it into three sections. The second floor, where the woman is speaking to Buzzi, falls 10 feet and begins to slide away. Buzzi is already out the door with a large florescent lantern, struggling through the water, following the piece of house with his neighbor inside. Twenty minutes later, he returns to his own home and his frightened fiancée, Melissa Griffith, with the drenched woman in tow.

In Seaside Heights the surge swamps Heiring Avenue, Carteret, Sampson, Sheridan and Sherman virtually simultaneously. At police headquarters, the floodwaters breach the first floor of the two-story building. Everyone, including roughly 60 residents of Seaside Heights who have taken shelter there, scrambles up to the second floor. Boyd worries about the generator washing away. It's the only thing powering his department. Hunkered down, the officers and homeowners spend a sleepless night listening to the screeching wind as it claws at the roof trying to pry if off.

A CRUEL DAWN

By midnight, however, the worst is over. By dawn, unfortunately, it is visible.

Splintered homes have floated out to sea. Others have come to rest on other streets and at crazy angles, like so many Monopoly houses and hotels.

Far to the north, water has filled the downtown area of Hoboken like it's a bathtub. Trees and utility poles all over the state snap and crack through the night, sending live wires, sparking and sizzling, across sidewalks, streets and lawns. Brief, arcing flames from severed power lines and blown transformers mimic lightning in the night sky, confusing some residents. Fractured gas mains spew clouds of the stuff into the swirling surge waters, which bubble ominously, and natural gas fires burn from Bay Head to Brick and Long Beach Island, some for as many as three days.

By Tuesday afternoon, Sandy is escorted out of the state by a slew of gray clouds stumbling drunkenly across the Northeast. Not until Wednesday does the sun make a welcome appearance.

Chief Boyd remains trapped at police headquarters in Seaside, until the floodwaters recede enough on Tuesday morning. It's 9 p.m. before he goes home for the first time in 48 hours.

Before he does, though, he tours his broken borough and the island where his family has lived since 1933.

Casino Pier, which he calls the anchor of town, is shattered. Debris is everywhere. Yet all across the state, the heavy equipment that will help rebuild New Jersey rumbles forward.

At the boardwalk, though — or what's left of it — it's quiet, except for the wind whipping the shredded fabric of Funtown, the ever-present pounding of the waves and the cawing of seabirds as they dip and dive and soar, reeling across the sky as if on some invisible ride.

NOTES: The story was written by Amy Ellis Nutt and primarily reported by James Queally, Mark Di Ionno, Stephen Stirling, Erin O'Neill, Ryan Hutchins, Tom Haydon, Jarrett Renshaw, Julia Terruso and Eric Sagara. It includes contributions and details from more than 30 other reporters.

RIGHT: An East Orange police officer tapes off a scene where an aluminum storage shed was lifted by the gusty wind and was destroyed when it landed straddling a fence on Park Avenue in the city during Hurricane Sandy.

JERRY MCCREA/THE STAR-LEDGER

ABOVE: A teenage boy explores the flooded streets of Cape May as the hurricane approaches landfall on Monday, Oct. 29. ARISTIDE ECONOMOPOULOS/THE STAR-LEDGER

MONDAY, OCT. 29

- Hurricane Sandy slams the state on a scale never seen — pounding the Jersey Shore, flooding roads and highways, and paralyzing much of the Northeast.

- Schools and most businesses around the state are closed. Major roads and mass transit systems, including NJ Transit and PATH are shut down, including a portion of the Garden State Parkway. The Holland Tunnel is closed, and the George Washington Bridge is closed to large vehicles.

- President Obama signs emergency declarations for New Jersey as well as six other states and the District of Columbia, allowing the states and the capital to request federal funds to help pay for recovery costs.

- The storm surge tears apart some of the state's most popular boardwalks in many resort communities, including a portion of the Funtown Pier in Seaside Heights.

- Christie blasts Atlantic City Mayor Lorenzo Langford for not heeding his directive to evacuate residents well in advance of the approaching storm.

- Police shut down the Mathis and Mantoloking bridges, blocking direct access to Seaside Heights.

ABOVE: Seaside Park's FunTown Pier takes a pounding on Monday evening, Oct. 29. DAVID GARD/THE STAR-LEDGER

LEFT: Waves crash over the dunes at Bridges Ave. as Hurricane Sandy makes its way toward Bay Head. JOHN MUNSON/THE STAR-LEDGER

OPPOSITE RIGHT: Gov. Chris Christie is surrounded by members of his cabinet during an evening news briefing on the status of Hurricane Sandy at the State Police Regional Operations Intelligence Center. TONY KURDZUK/THE STAR-LEDGER

RIGHT: Manasquan firefighter Kevin Richie tries to gain entry to a home to rescue trapped residents. ANDREW MILLS/THE STAR-LEDGER

BELOW: Firefighters wade through waist-high water to rescue trapped residents from homes in **Manasquan.** ANDREW MILLS/THE STAR-LEDGER

OPPOSITE: On Tuesday, Oct. 30, a Raritan Yacht Club member tries to get a hold on the destruction caused to members' boats and the club by Hurricane Sandy in **Perth Amboy.** FRANCES MICKLOW/THE STAR-LEDGER

FOLLOWING RIGHT: Members of the Cape May Department of Public Works clean storm drains to try to stop the flooding. ARISTIDE ECONOMOPOULOS/THE STAR-LEDGER

GO TO NJ.COM FOR LIVE UPDATES ON THE STORM

PUMMELED

Storm surge slams Shore from Cape May to Seaside Heights

Christie warns those who refused to leave to hunker down

DAVID GARD/THE STAR-LEDGER

A wall of sea foam rushes down the boardwalk as Hurricane Sandy strikes Seaside Heights yesterday. The storm turned part of Funtown Pier into a pile of wooden beams and twisted fencing.

In the midst of a storm, a tempest between governor and mayor

To our readers

Final production and printing of this edition was delayed. It is being delivered to satisfy reader demand. The content for this edition was filed Monday and the paper's editorial production was nearing

By Ted Sherman / STAR-LEDGER STAFF

Hurricane Sandy, now a storm for the record books, hit New Jersey with an unrelenting fury last night, slamming the state on a scale never before seen — pounding the Jersey Shore, flooding roads and highways, and

CHAPTER FOUR

The Aftermath

ABOVE: A boat comes to rest on Perth Amboy's storm-tattered brick boardwalk along Water Street Oct. 30.
CHRIS FAYTOK/THE STAR-LEDGER

LEFT: A fallen tree lies on the lawn outside a home on Liberty Street in Fords. CHRIS FAYTOK/THE STAR-LEDGER

ABOVE: Vehicles brave the floodwaters on Route 46 in Little Ferry Oct. 30. WILLIAM PERLMAN/THE STAR-LEDGER

ABOVE: Widespread devastation along Brook (top) and Prospect avenues in Union Beach after Hurricane Sandy destroyed areas of the Jersey Shore. ANDREW MILLS/THE STAR-LEDGER

LEFT: Joseph Zayas returns to his home in Union Beach Oct. 30. He painted the sign to reassure concerned friends and family members.
ED MURRAY/THE STAR-LEDGER

ABOVE: Jerry Cerlipione rides his bicycle on the beach in Point Pleasant Beach Oct. 30. JOHN MUNSON/THE STAR-LEDGER

RIGHT: Boats tossed about by the storm sit atop the Brielle Road drawbridge on the Manasquan beachfront. ANDREW MILLS/THE STAR-LEDGER

BELOW: State Police, members of the National Guard and Secaucus firefighters rescue families from their homes on Edstan Drive in Moonachie. WILLIAM PERLMAN/THE STAR-LEDGER

TUESDAY, OCT. 30

- An unprecedented storm surge in the Raritan Bay and up the Hudson River pushes seawater into places it had never gone.
- Parts of many towns throughout the state remained underwater, including Moonachie, Sayreville, Hoboken and Jersey City.
- Statewide, more than 2.7 million homes and businesses are without power. Utility officials warn it could take up to 10 days to complete restoration.
- NJ Transit train and bus service remains suspended.
- The FunTown Pier is demolished in Seaside Park. In Seaside Heights, the Atlantic claimed the Casino Pier, its roller coaster left a twisted mass of metal in the ocean.

TOP RIGHT: The roller coaster from Casino Pier sits in the ocean in Seaside Heights Oct. 30.

DAVID GARD/THE STAR-LEDGER

BOTTOM RIGHT: A view of Lyman Street in Mantoloking after the storm surge cut a new inlet from Barnegat Bay to the Atlantic Ocean.

JOHN MUNSON/THE STAR-LEDGER

ABOVE: An SUV can be seen in the intersection of Brielle Road and First Avenue in Manasquan after the morning high tide recedes.

ABOVE: Mike Wickman, who owns Mike's Balloon Water Gun Game, and his wife, Debra Wickman, talk with Marylynn Falk amid the ruins of Keansburg Amusement Park on Oct. 30. ED MURRAY/THE STAR-LEDGER

ABOVE: What's left of a home stands in Union Beach Oct. 30. ED MURRAY/THE STAR-LEDGER

LEFT: A toy and a cash register lie side by side at Keansburg Amusement Park. ED MURRAY/THE STAR-LEDGER

FOLLOWING LEFT: Teresa Leverock looks into a room at the home of Heather Cosoleto in Union Beach. ED MURRAY/THE STAR-LEDGER

FOLLOWING TOP RIGHT: Heather Cosoleto, left, tries to recover a bag from her living room. ED MURRAY/THE STAR-LEDGER

FOLLOWING BOTTOM RIGHT: Pete Majoras of Point Pleasant looks at what used to be Lyman Street in Mantoloking before stormwaters washed over it. JOHN MUNSON/THE STAR-LEDGER

ABOVE: Marco Robles and his son Derick, 7, try to relax at the shelter in the Sayreville Senior Center Oct. 30. Hurricane Sandy flooded the basement and first floor of their home and left it without power. FRANCES MICKLOW/THE STAR-LEDGER

RIGHT: Evacuated Seaside Heights resident Jean Sabino tries to cope staying at a temporary shelter at Toms River High School East. NOAH K. MURRAY/THE STAR-LEDGER

FAR RIGHT: Edy Pagoda phones a friend to talk about the Boardwalk in Atlantic City as he stands amid what's left of it.

NOAH K. MURRAY/THE STAR-LEDGER

ABOVE: A home stands swamped on a Leonardo street Oct. 30.
ED MURRAY/THE STAR-LEDGER

OPPOSITE: Sand covers the steps leading to the boardwalk in Sea Isle City. ARISTIDE ECONOMOPOULOS/THE STAR-LEDGER

BELOW: A long line of people wait to fill gas cans at the Delta station in Roselle Park. JOHN O'BOYLE/THE STAR-LEDGER

The Star-Ledger

$1.00 | WEDNESDAY, OCTOBER 31, 2012   FINAL EDITION

NJ.COM

HISTORIC DEVASTATION

Monster storm leaves destruction throughout the state, millions without power and a still-rising death toll

DAVID GARD/THE STAR-LEDGER

Debris litters the beach at Seaside Heights while what remains of the Casino Pier teeters in the background yesterday, less than one day after Hurricane Sandy crashed into the state.

TO OUR READERS

Publishing today's edition of The Star-Ledger was a unique challenge. We moved our newsroom three times yesterday because of power and internet outages. Our building in Newark went dark at 8:55 Monday night, and as of our press start last night, we were still without power for our editorial, advertising and circulation staffs.

Throughout the storm, we had teams of reporters, photographers and videographers reporting around the

By Mark Mueller and Ted Sherman
STAR-LEDGER STAFF

C alamitous. Incalculable. Unthinkable. New Jersey officials and residents have run out of words to describe the damage wrought by Hurricane Sandy, a behemoth of a storm that more than lived up to its hype.

Up and down the coast, the ocean roared ashore, dislodging homes from their foundations, ripping away piers, swallowing entire neighborhoods, and leaving millions in the dark — many who are now being told to expect to remain without power for a week or longer.

With a full accounting yet to be

people in seven states — 16 in New York City. Another 69 people were killed in the Caribbean, before Hurricane Sandy veered north along the East Coast.

"I think the losses are going to be almost incalculable," said Gov. Chris Christie yesterday, as daylight brought graphic testimony to the damage and devastation caused by a record-setting storm

WEDNESDAY, OCT. 31

- Across the state, long lines of frustrated motorists snake for blocks leading to the few gas stations open for business.
- The number of New Jersey deaths blamed on what is now the biggest storm on record grows daily.
- President Obama accompanies Gov. Chris Christie on a nearly hour long helicopter tour of the Shore areas hardest hit by Sandy.
- The waterfront community of Lavallette and the Ortley Beach section and other beachfront portions of Toms River are nearly indistinguishable from one another due to the wreckage.
- On Long Beach Island, where authorities got their first look at the fallout from the storm, houses were still flooded and vehicles were lodged on porches.

ABOVE: Cars make their way around debris on Raymond Boulevard in Newark.
JENNIFER BROWN/THE STAR-LEDGER

LEFT: Jose Gomes, owner of Elsy Auto Repair on Raymond Boulevard in Newark, gingerly makes his way through his shop, where water levels reached about 4 feet high and bent the steel door. JENNIFER BROWN/THE STAR-LEDGER

ABOVE: Crews work to restore power lines at Douglas Street and Route 37 on Oct. 31 in Toms River. SAED HINDASH/THE STAR-LEDGER

LEFT: Home Depot manager Robert Jakium, center, helps distribute portable generators to a throng of shoppers. ROBERT SCIARRINO/THE STAR-LEDGER

BOTTOM LEFT: Marcus Krison of Randolph joins a line of motorists waiting to purchase gas at the Shell station on Route 10 east in Succasunna. Owner Jerry Riccardello said he was almost out of gas and was told by his supplier there would not be any delivered for the next two days. ROBERT SCIARRINO/THE STAR-LEDGER

BOTTOM RIGHT: Heidi Pfleger looks at a neighbor's boat that ended up in her backyard in the Beach Haven West section of Stafford Township. NOAH K. MURRAY/THE STAR-LEDGER

ABOVE: Making the most of their time off from school, Devon Welborn, left, and Emily Barling, both 9, and Dylan Welborn, 7, became entrepreneurs when downed trees increased traffic in their Byram neighborhood. They set up a stand selling hot chocolate, gum and candy and were pleased with their sales. JERRY MCCREA/THE STAR-LEDGER

RIGHT: Molly Sullivan, 8, of Scotch Plains shows her feelings about Halloween trick-or-treating being postponed. Instead, children on Montague Street marked the holiday by wearing their costumes as they played outside. ED MURRAY/THE STAR-LEDGER

ABOVE: Gov. Chris Christie greets President Obama and Federal Emergency Management Agency Administrator Craig Fugate before an aerial tour of the damage Oct. 31. TIM LARSEN/GOV. CHRISTIE'S OFFICE

LEFT: Christie, Obama and Fugate exit the helicopters at Atlantic City Airport after the tour. TIM LARSEN/GOV. CHRISTIE'S OFFICE

FAR LEFT: The calm after the storm in the Beach Haven West section of Stafford Township. NOAH K. MURRAY/THE STAR-LEDGER

ABOVE: National Guard troops help evacuate a woman and baby who had been stranded in their Hoboken home.

JENNIFER BROWN/THE STAR-LEDGER

RIGHT: Smashed boats sit in a heap at Brennan Boat Company & Marina on Route 70 in Brick Oct. 31.

ANDREW MILLS/THE STAR-LEDGER

The Star-Ledger

$1.00 | THURSDAY, NOVEMBER 1, 2012

nj.com

FINAL EDITION
++

GO TO NJ.COM FOR UP-TO-THE-MINUTE COVERAGE

PURE HELL

Sandy leaves state with neighborhoods underwater, at least 12 dead, massive power outages, fears of gas shortages

By Ted Sherman / STAR-LEDGER STAFF

Mantoloking was a war zone of ruined houses and isolated fires.

The National Guard delivered relief supplies and evacuated residents in Hoboken.

Across the state, long lines of frustrated motorists snaked for blocks leading to the few gas stations open for business, while tempers flared. Millions spent another day without power — or heat in their homes — with no expectations of getting it back anytime soon.

And the number of New Jersey deaths blamed on what is now the biggest storm on record grew to at least 12 last night when authorities said two Newark sisters, ages 18 and 19, died of carbon monoxide poisoning after keeping a generator too close to their home.

Even as New Jersey struggled for normalcy, the scope and intensity of devastation waged by the superstorm that began in the Caribbean as Hurricane Sandy only grew yesterday as new pictures and videos painted a post-apocalyptic landscape from Cape May through the state's barrier islands and beyond.

From the air, it looked like a nuclear bomb had hit.

From wealthy suburban communities in the north, betrayed by their stately trees that took down power lines and smashed homes and cars,

SEE **SANDY**, PAGE 26

15 hurricane pages inside

BARRIERS BROKEN
A town-by-town breakdown of the damage on the hard-hit coast. Page 25

CLEANUP COSTS
The lessons of Hurricane Katrina may help the state deal with the budget hit from the storm. Page 27

OFFICIAL VISITS
President Obama joins Gov. Chris Christie on a tour of devastated Shore communities. Page 28

NEED HELP? A guide to help you survive power outages, begin repairs and get assistance. Page 35

Business losses may add $30B to N.J. expense list

By Ed Beeson and Tom De Poto
STAR-LEDGER STAFF

The damage from Hurricane Sandy will likely exceed that from Tropical Storm Irene, but the cost to businesses could be far worse.

Analysts estimate property damage along the Eastern Seaboard could be as much as $20 billion, but say business losses could reach as high as

ABOVE: Huge pumps are used along Observer Highway to help relieve the flooding in Hoboken.

JENNIFER BROWN/THE STAR-LEDGER

BELOW: National Guard troops evacuate a woman on a stretcher.

JENNIFER BROWN/THE STAR-LEDGER

When Sandy Hit | 85

ABOVE: Route 35 north in Ortley Beach is covered in sand and debris as crews weave between power lines to begin cleaning up. SAED HINDASH/THE STAR-LEDGER

ABOVE: Gary Sona surveys the damage from the roof of his flooded home in the Laurence Harbor section of Old Bridge Oct. 31. FRANCES MICKLOW/THE STAR-LEDGER

ABOVE: James Indelicato comforts his weeping wife, Jennifer West-Indelicato, as they go through their Laurence Harbor home for the first time after the storm flooded it. There was still water in the streets of Cliffwood Way two days later. FRANCES MICKLOW/THE STAR-LEDGER

LEFT: A car is buried in sand at Carolina Avenue and Long Beach Boulevard in the Holgate section of Long Beach Island. NOAH K. MURRAY/THE STAR-LEDGER

FAR LEFT: Contractor Ron Kessler cleans the sand out of the first floor foyer of Charles Caucci's Central Avenue home in Ocean City. About 3 feet of water filled the house, bringing with it piles of sand. ARISTIDE ECONOMOPOULOS/THE STAR-LEDGER

ABOVE: Horicio Cartagena, center, waits for his phone to finish charging at the ShopRite in Jersey City, one of the few places in the city with power. The supermarket let people plug in their phones and computers in the lobby. JENNIFER BROWN/THE STAR-LEDGER

LEFT: A home is knocked off its foundation in Normandy Beach.
SAED HINDASH/THE STAR-LEDGER

FAR LEFT: Beach Haven resident Jim McMahon, viewing the destruction Oct. 31, said he couldn't believe the damage Hurricane Sandy caused in Holgate on Long Beach Island.

NOAH K. MURRAY/THE STAR-LEDGER

ABOVE: The stairs are the only thing remaining of the boardwalk in Ocean City. ARISTIDE ECONOMOPOULOS/THE STAR-LEDGER

RIGHT: Seaside Heights Police Chief Thomas Boyd points to the collapsed Jet Star roller coaster and the surrounding debris near the Casino Pier during a tour on Oct. 31. DAVID GARD/THE STAR-LEDGER

ABOVE: A boat on Oct. 31 investigates a house in the middle of Barnegat Bay near Mantoloking, apparently washed away by Hurricane Sandy. ANDREW MILLS/THE STAR-LEDGER

LEFT: Seaside Heights on the day after Hurricane Sandy landed. DAVID GARD/THE STAR-LEDGER

RIGHT: A man looks over the wreckage on the Seaside Heights beach near Casino Pier on Oct. 31. DAVID GARD/THE STAR-LEDGER

OPPOSITE: The Ferris wheel towers over the remains of the FunTown Pier in Seaside Park. DAVID GARD/THE STAR-LEDGER

BOTTOM LEFT: Residents walk over a sand-covered street in the Holgate section of Long Beach Island. NOAH K. MURRAY/THE STAR-LEDGER

BOTTOM RIGHT: A bike is stuck in sand in the garage of Charlie Caucci's Central Avenue home in Ocean City. ARISTIDE ECONOMOPOULOS/THE STAR-LEDGER

ABOVE: Kim Tkacs, right, a registered nurse with the Medical Resource Corp., helps Frank Antalec, his wife, Sui Ling Xu, their 9-month-old daughter, Emma Lanhua Antalec, and his mother, Rose Antalec, as the family prepares to take shelter at the Mennen Arena in Morris Township Oct. 31.

ROBERT SCIARRINO/THE STAR-LEDGER

ABOVE: An aerial view of the devastation in Ortley Beach Oct. 31.

ANDREW MILLS/THE STAR-LEDGER

LEFT: A man stands in knee-deep water outside Legal Beans in Hoboken.

WILLIAM PERLMAN/THE STAR-LEDGER

ABOVE: Solders carry a child out of a rescue vehicle as the National Guard continues its operation in Hoboken Oct. 31.
WILLIAM PERLMAN/THE STAR-LEDGER

RIGHT: Residents along Grand Street in Jersey City clean out their basement apartments. JENNIFER BROWN/THE STAR-LEDGER

FAR RIGHT: A man walks behind cars swamped by floodwaters on a street in Hoboken.
WILLIAM PERLMAN/THE STAR-LEDGER

ABOVE: Neighbors Eddie Aumack and Tara Lee try to get a fire going to warm themselves and dry their clothing in Union Beach Oct. 31. ED MURRAY/THE STAR-LEDGER

LEFT: Fires smolder in the South Mantoloking section of Brick Township. Natural gas fires burned for days along the barrier islands. ANDREW MILLS/THE STAR-LEDGER

ABOVE: People look at a house that landed in a field in Union Beach.

ED MURRAY/THE STAR-LEDGER

RIGHT: Justin Shelton of Remediation Specialists Contracting makes repairs to a flooded home off William Street in Sayreville Oct. 31.

FRANCES MICKLOW/THE STAR-LEDGER

FAR RIGHT: Angela Ciangiotto tries the phone as her daughter Renee Adams gazes over the fence where their clothes are drying in their Union Beach yard.

ED MURRAY/THE STAR-LEDGER

ABOVE: Scott Kautzmann of Succasunna found this old family photo in a puddle at the former home of his grandparents in Chadwick Beach on the Barnegat Bay Nov. 1. Kautzmann, who spent much of his childhood at the home, took a boat to see how it fared in the storm. The house, which now belongs to his mother, Diane, initially appeared undamaged, but he discovered about 3 feet of water inside. JOHN MUNSON/THE STAR-LEDGER

LEFT: A view of Brook Avenue in Union Beach on Nov. 1. ED MURRAY/THE STAR-LEDGER

FOLLOWING LEFT: This house sits in the middle of a new inlet off the Mantoloking Bridge on Oct. 31. ANDREW MILLS/THE STAR-LEDGER

FOLLOWING RIGHT: Mary Colasurdo and Marcia Slekitis help a friend retrieve valuables from the foundation of her home in the Bayville section of Berkeley Township Nov. 1. Lisa Kwabis returned to her home to find it had been ripped from the foundation and washed 200 feet away, landing half on land, half in a lagoon. DAVID GARD/THE STAR-LEDGER

THURSDAY, NOV. 1

- Gas is nearly impossible to find in many areas. Police stand watch over angry customers.
- Many streets remain impassible, schools shuttered, businesses still closed.
- The National Weather Service warns of another nor'easter coming next week.
- More than 1.7 million customers remain without power. Gov. Chris Christie tells state utility leaders they need to come up with a better plan to restore service.
- The Department of Defense flies in 17 aircraft from California, loaded with power-generation equipment, bucket trucks and crews provided by Southern California power companies to help restore power.
- The long wait for power means many people turn to emergency generators, leading to new tragedies, deaths from carbon monoxide poisoning.
- NJ Transit buses are back, where roads are open. Newark Liberty International Airport is fully operational and airlines are increasing service. Subways also start running again in parts of New York City.

TOP RIGHT: A handmade sign tells the story at a gas station in Rockaway Nov. 1.

JERRY MCCREA/THE STAR-LEDGER

BOTTOM RIGHT: Thomas Hermley-Keen, an employee of 80 West Exxon in Rockaway, puts diesel fuel into an ambulance from St. Clare's Hospital. The station where he works ran out of gasoline, and was only dispensing its remaining diesel to local ambulance crews.

JERRY MCCREA/THE STAR-LEDGER

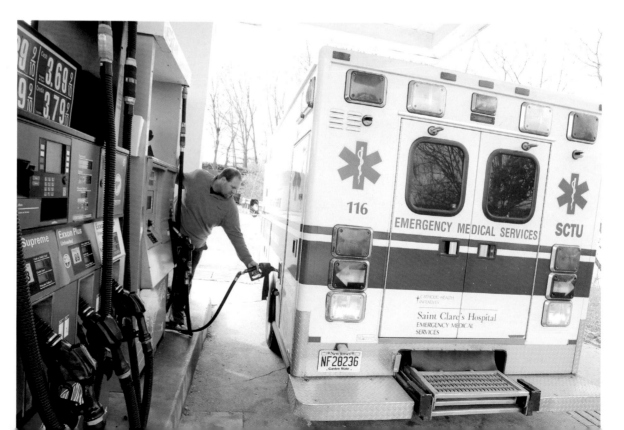

LEFT: Ice and other supplies are distributed at Holy Family School on Route 36 in Union Beach Nov. 1.

ED MURRAY/THE STAR-LEDGER

BOTTOM LEFT: Sisters Kelly Deangelo and Denise Zitzman struggle as they carry two giant bags of ice from the distribution center at Holy Family.

ED MURRAY/THE STAR-LEDGER

BOTTOM RIGHT: Belmar resident Mark Heuth paddles through floodwaters on Ninth St. in Belmar with his 4-year-old son, Hunter, and 9-year-old daughter, Madelyn.

TONY KURDZUK/THE STAR-LEDGER

ABOVE: Jim and Robin Bedaro of Waretown look out at the Barnegat Bay. They came out to help the Becker family with their heavily damaged home Nov. 1. DAVID GARD/THE STAR-LEDGER

LEFT: The relative of a neighbor looks over the remains of Lisa Kwabis' home in the Bayville section of Berkeley Township. The home was ripped from its foundation and washed 200 feet away, landing half on land, half in a lagoon. DAVID GARD/THE STAR-LEDGER

ABOVE: Blair Carswell of Jersey City looks at his car, which was completely submerged by the water that moved swiftly through the city.

JENNIFER BROWN/THE STAR-LEDGER

OPPOSITE: Belmar resident Ed McCormick paddles his canoe through the intersection of Ninth Avenue and E Street Nov. 1.

TONY KURDZUK/THE STAR-LEDGER

BELOW: With gas cans in hand, Sharon Palmer, right, and more than 30 others wait patiently in line for fuel for their generators at the R.C.S. service station on Washington Street in Boonton.

ROBERT SCIARRINO/THE STAR-LEDGER

$1.00 | FINAL EDITION

The Star-Ledger

FRIDAY, NOVEMBER 2, 2012

We will come back.

A flag stands as a sign of resolve beside devastated homes on Brook Avenue in Union Beach yesterday.

ED MURRAY/THE STAR-LEDGER

THE WRECKAGE WILL BE CLEARED, THE SAND PUSHED BACK WHERE IT BELONGS.

Mark Di Ionno
nj.com/diionno

New boards will be nailed down, new pavilions constructed. The barrier islands will be re-overbuilt, just like always. And sometime before Memorial Day, Gov. Christie will announce, "The Jersey Shore is open for business."

It has to be.

The Jersey Shore generates most of the state's $38 billion tourism industry.

And it will be.

Because it is our most valuable resource, natural and otherwise, on levels that go so much deeper than money. The ocean is soothing, when not raging. The shore breezes cool us, when not uproot-

typhoon winds pushed high tide to record heights and sent ocean-like waves crashing over seawalls and bulkheads.

In our dark, cold homes and our gas lines and long waits at whatever food store or restaurant has power, we're still standing.

Maybe Christie said it best.

"This is the kind of thing New Jerseyans are built for — we're

said Thomas Boyd, the Seaside Heights police chief, as he stood on a 5-foot sand mound in the middle of Route 35. "But we're going to start."

In front of him was a yellow Cape Cod, broken in three sections, one of thousands upon thousands of homes destroyed or damaged in the 12-hour height of Sandy's fury.

described when her mood turned from shock to resolve.

She said this standing in front of town hall, wearing muddy knee-high rubber boots and dirty yellow work gloves, as she worked with about 125 residents picking up limbs, branches and the town's boardwalk, a mile of which was rebuilt after Tropical Storm Irene. Now all two miles are gone. Every board, pounded

PLEASE FEEL FREE TO CHARGE YOUR PHONE.

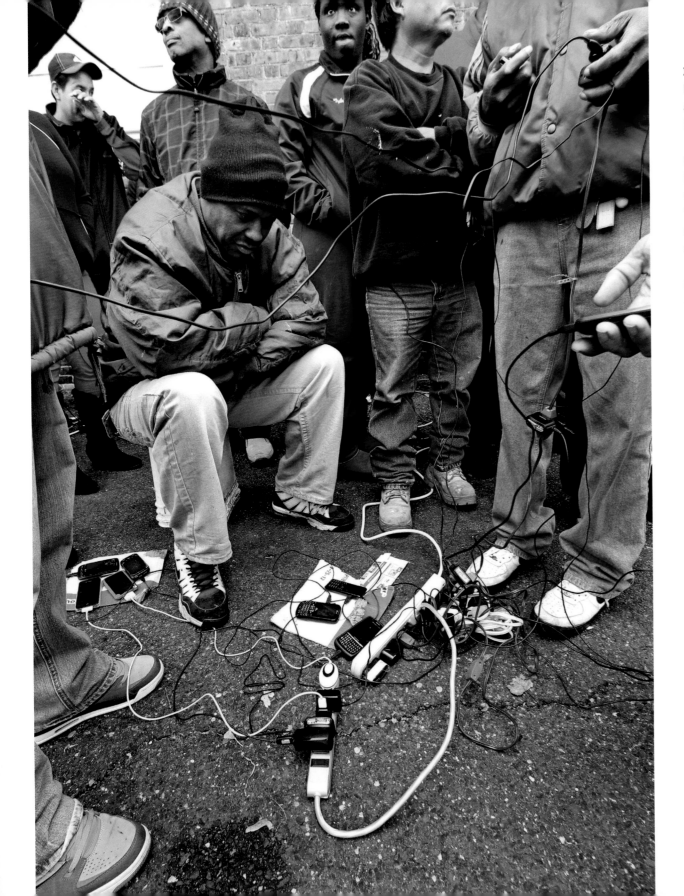

LEFT: John Holmes finally gets to charge his cell phone after waiting seven hours at the firehouse on Main Street in Asbury Park Nov. 1. NOAH K. MURRAY/THE STAR-LEDGER

OPPOSITE TOP: Asbury Park residents line up in front of the firehouse for a chance to charge their cell phones. The fire department placed power lines outside to help people without electricity. NOAH K. MURRAY/THE STAR-LEDGER

OPPOSITE BOTTOM LEFT: Some good Samaritans who got their power back along Hudson Street in Hoboken ran electrical cords and power strips so neighbors, including Jason Monico, pictured, could charge their phones and computers. JENNIFER BROWN/THE STAR-LEDGER

OPPOSITE BOTTOM RIGHT: The good Samaritans of Hoboken even put out chairs and provided snacks for their neighbors. JENNIFER BROWN/THE STAR-LEDGER

LEFT: Tony Rodrigues of Lodi lifts debris into a bucket loader in front of the Howard Roland Pavilion in Belmar.

TONY KURDZUK/THE STAR-LEDGER

FAR LEFT: More evidence of Sandy's devastation in Sea Bright, where the business district was hit hard.

ARISTIDE ECONOMOPOULOS/THE STAR-LEDGER

BOTTOM LEFT: The roof off Donovan's Tree House Bar lies in the roadway in Sea Bright Nov. 1.

ARISTIDE ECONOMOPOULOS/THE STAR-LEDGER

BOTTOM RIGHT: The hollowed-out remains of the lifeguard station in the Howard Roland Pavilion.

TONY KURDZUK/THE STAR-LEDGER

ABOVE: Cindy Claus, director at Jenkinson's Aquarium in Point Pleasant Beach, checks out Seaquin the seal. Eight employees rode out the storm at the aquarium to ensure the safety of the animals. SAED HINDASH/THE STAR-LEDGER

ABOVE: Verizon workers replace eight utility poles that snapped in the storm, on Friday Nov. 2 along Route 130 southbound in South Brunswick.

PATTI SAPONE/THE STAR-LEDGER

FRIDAY, NOV. 2

- Gov. Chris Christie announces that odd-even gas rationing will start in 12 counties.

- Plans are under way to increase gasoline deliveries and provide portable generators to stations equipped to hook up emergency power supplies.

- All natural gas on the barrier islands is turned off because many lines ruptured when the hurricane ripped homes off their foundations, causing major fires. At least 20 homes burned to the ground in Mantoloking.

- Local police departments order mandatory evacuations of Seaside Heights, Seaside Park, island sections of Berkeley Township including South Seaside Park, Lavallette, Ortley Beach and Mantoloking. Residents may not be allowed back for up to eight months.

- Christie says the state will build a temporary bridge over a newly formed inlet that cut Mantoloking in half so that cleanup crews can get to the northern portion of the town.

- Soldiers from the National Guard join officers from the Monmouth County sheriff's and prosecutor's offices to patrol neighborhoods in coastal towns in the county, hit hard by the storm.

- Atlantic City reopens for business.

RIGHT: Bayonne resident Osiris Wasef pushes his car past a closed gas station as he waits in line for hours to fill his tank. The line wrapped around several city blocks to reach the Valero gas station in Jersey City.

JENNIFER BROWN/THE STAR-LEDGER

ABOVE: John Canticas, the owner of the Speedway gas station in the Ironia section of Randolph, runs between pumps, which are powered by a generator he had to hire an electrician to install. Due to his limited supply of fuel, he is forced to restrict customers to a purchase of $40, cash only because he does not have the power to run credit cards.
ROBERT SCIARRINO/THE STAR-LEDGER

BELOW: A Mobile Satellite Emergency Department is set up in a parking lot of Ocean Medical Center in Brick to take the overflow from busy emergency rooms. It is one of the two MSEDs in the state; the other is in Hoboken. TONY KURDZUK/THE STAR-LEDGER

ABOVE: Members of the Randolph Police Department keep things calm as drivers desperate for gas buy the maximum $40 worth of fuel in cash at the Speedway gas station in Ironia. Similar scenes played out across the state, particularly in the central and northern counties placed under rationing. ROBERT SCIARRINO/THE STAR-LEDGER

RIGHT: Hoboken Patrolman William Oquendo comforts Amare Griffin, 4, as officers help pass out free ice and water provided by PSE&G. JENNIFER BROWN/THE STAR-LEDGER

ABOVE: Workers repair a water main outside an apartment building in Hoboken. JENNIFER BROWN/THE STAR-LEDGER

LEFT: Hoboken Residents try to get back to normal even as water and mud still cover the streets. JENNIFER BROWN/THE STAR-LEDGER

FAR LEFT: Left to right, Max Waitz, Christopher Damaskos and Jack Waitz offer lollipops, water and pretzels to motorists and take donations for the Red Cross while at a gas line for the Lukoil in Upper Montclair. Drivers waited at least two-and-a-half hours to get to the pump. FRANCES MICKLOW/THE STAR-LEDGER

ABOVE: Three swans look for handouts next to a damaged dock behind a home on Seagoin Road in the Cherry Quay section of Brick, where the homeowner would regularly feed them. TONY KURDZUK/THE STAR-LEDGER

RIGHT: Susan Smith tries to climb over a section of her dock that ended up in the alley beside her house on Seagoin Road in Cherry Quay. She and her husband, Ken, encountered Hurricane Sandy twice — first when they were on vacation in Jamaica and again after they returned home. TONY KURDZUK/THE STAR-LEDGER

ABOVE: Brick residents Ronald Lesczynski (front) and his son-in-law, Matt Spainhoward, stand in the back of a pickup truck in order to dump their garbage on the top of an overflowing Dumpster at the Drum Point Elementary School. The Dumpsters were put in place because township sanitation trucks were not able to navigate all the streets in town. TONY KURDZUK/THE STAR-LEDGER

BELOW: At least one motorist plans to make the most of his trip to the Lukoil gas station in Upper Montclair, bringing gas cans with him. Across the state, the orange cans, used to fuel generators, became a common sight.

FRANCES MICKLOW/THE STAR-LEDGER

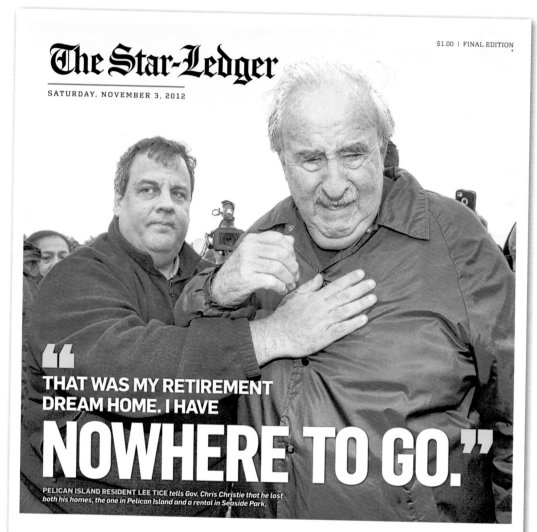

The Star-Ledger

$1.00 | FINAL EDITION

SATURDAY, NOVEMBER 3, 2012

" **THAT WAS MY RETIREMENT DREAM HOME. I HAVE NOWHERE TO GO."**

PELICAN ISLAND RESIDENT LEE TICE *tells Gov. Chris Christie that he lost both his homes, the one in Pelican Island and a rental in Seaside Park.*

As gas shortage grows, rationing imposed in 12 counties

7 towns on barrier islands to be evacuated for months

By Ted Sherman / STAR-LEDGER STAFF

Authorities ordered a mandatory evacuation of one section of New Jersey's shoreline last night, and Gov. Chris Christie announced odd-even gas rationing as the Garden State continues to reel from the aftereffects of Hurricane Sandy.

Across the state, power company workers struggled to piece back together the complex electric grid left tangled and twisted by Monday's monster storm. They worked to untangle miles and miles of mangled, burnt-out wires — along roads, amid shattered trees, blocked-off intersections and local power substations.

Five days after Hurricane Sandy slammed into New Jersey, some 1.6 million customers — more than a third of all homes and businesses — remained without electricity.

No juice means gas stations can't pump gas. And after another day of long lines of people waiting to fill up, as tanks and tempers

TOP: TONY KURDZUK/THE STAR-LEDGER; ABOVE: DAVID GARD/THE STAR-LEDGER

A convoy of rescue crews leaves Seaside Heights yesterday evening. Residents who were still in the town reported that police and fire officials gave them just minutes to pack their bags and leave, after a mandatory evacuation was declared.

Amid horror, death-defying heroism, simple acts of kindness by strangers

By Kelly Heyboer and Victoria St. Martin
STAR-LEDGER STAFF

It began with a late-night chat after seeing Hurricane Sandy's devastation unfolding in New

Mich. "We said, 'Let's do it and let's do it now.' We figured, let's get in a truck and get on our way to New Jersey."

Yesterday, he and a police offi-

WHERE TO GET HELP

From filing

ABOVE: Hoboken residents congregate in the large tent that is the PSE&G command center on Washington Street to get something to eat and drink while they charge their phone and other electronics. JENNIFER BROWN/THE STAR-LEDGER

ABOVE: Area residents deliver donations of food and clothing for evacuated Seaside Heights residents staying at Toms River High School East, a temporary shelter.

NOAH K. MURRAY/THE STAR-LEDGER

RIGHT: A convoy of rescue vehicles leaves Seaside Heights on Friday evening, Nov. 2.

DAVID GARD/THE STAR-LEDGER

FAR RIGHT: The view from the Jersey City waterfront shows a partially lit New York City skyline during power outages across the city. JENNIFER BROWN/THE STAR-LEDGER

TOP: Point Pleasant Beach varsity football players walk down Chicago Avenue as the team gets together to help clean up the area. TONY KURDZUK/THE STAR-LEDGER

ABOVE: Tim Morris looks back at a dining room set he helped carry to the curb from a home on Parkway. Members of the team helped neighbors clean up on Saturday, Nov. 3, five days after Sandy hit. TONY KURDZUK/THE STAR-LEDGER

LEFT: Football player Josh Lang stacks soaked documents on top of a TV in the home of Eileen Levis.

TONY KURDZUK/THE STAR-LEDGER

SATURDAY, NOV. 3

- Some trains are rolling again. Schools are expected to open next week. "We need to think forward," Gov. Chris Christie said, "about how we return to normalcy."

- Odd-even gas rationing is instituted in 12 counties: Bergen, Essex, Hudson, Hunterdon, Middlesex, Morris, Monmouth, Passaic, Somerset, Sussex, Union and Warren.

- Utility crews continue to arrive from across the country. In total, New Jersey will have 11,000 workers repairing lines and restoring substations.

- The Federal Emergency Management Agency opens comfort centers in hard-hit areas, giving residents a chance to warm up, power their electronic equipment and watch television.

- In Manasquan, homeowners are permitted to retrieve belongings from their houses after first showing proof of residency.

- Access to barrier islands remains cut off.

ABOVE: Five days after Hurricane Sandy, crews from the Morris Township Department of Public Works clean up Canfield Road, securing downed power lines and clearing fallen trees that have limited residents' movements.
ROBERT SCIARRINO/THE STAR-LEDGER

RIGHT: Stylist Joey Stagaard gives Lenny Mazzuca a trim at Toms River High School East, a temporary shelter for residents evacuated from Seaside Heights and other Shore communities. NOAH K. MURRAY/THE STAR-LEDGER

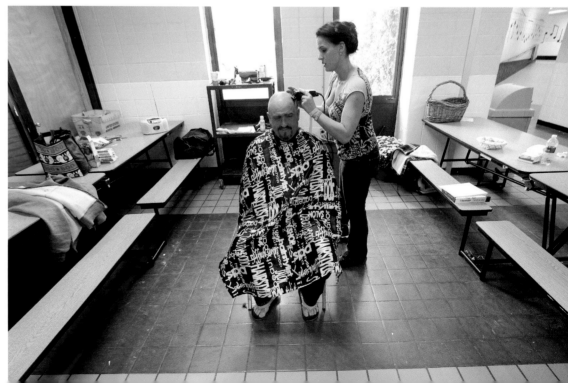

ABOVE AND LEFT: Red Cross workers provide hot meals to residents in Jersey City's devastated Country Village neighborhood. JENNIFER BROWN/THE STAR-LEDGER

ABOVE: Voters line up at the Ocean County Administration Building in Toms River on Saturday, Nov. 3, to get mail-in ballots for the Tuesday, Nov. 6., election. NOAH K. MURRAY/THE STAR-LEDGER

LEFT TOP: Contractors spray anti-mold agent as walls and fixtures are ripped out of Daniel Suriaga's Little Ferry home, which was hit with 3 feet of floodwaters from Hurricane Sandy. As the water rose, Suriaga and his wife rushed to rescue their three children who were asleep in the lower level of the bi-level home. ROBERT SCIARRINO/THE STAR-LEDGER

LEFT BOTTOM: Donated blankets for residents of Sea Bright affected by Hurricane Sandy are left out in Rumson on Saturday, Nov. 3. FRANCES MICKLOW/THE STAR-LEDGER

FAR LEFT: Hurricane Sandy sheared away half of a home on Front Street in Union Beach. TOMÁS DINGES/ THE STAR-LEDGER

Sunday Star-Ledger

SUNDAY, NOVEMBER 4, 2012

48 HOURS THAT FOREVER CHANGED NEW JERSEY

TONY KURDZUK/THE STAR-LEDGER

Rick Oliver of Berlin, Camden County, looks out at the water and clouds yesterday as he stands on a new berm pushed up by bulldozers on the Bay Head beach in Sandy's aftermath.

Sandy's devastation was widespread, but perhaps it resonated most along the Jersey Shore, where seemingly every family has made memories, where every kid has played Skee-Ball in a boardwalk arcade and where the sausage-and-pepper sandwiches tasted unlike anything we ever put in our mouths. This morning, there are only splinters where towns stood and there is a roller coaster in the Atlantic. The owners vow to rebuild, the residents to return. The resolve is the same everywhere you go, even as people struggle to understand what happened last week.

With that in mind, this is the blow-by-blow account of Sandy's deadly path into New Jersey. It was based on eyewitness accounts from Shore residents and officials, including many who rode out the storm on the barrier islands. Also included are meteorological data and interviews with officials who describe how the storm stalked the state for days before turning on New Jersey and unleashing a double-fisted fury beyond all imagining.

NOAH K. MURRAY/THE STAR-LEDGER

The face of Seaside Heights evacuee Jean Sabino expresses the emotions many are feeling as they try to cope.

Watch videos of the storm's impact at **nj.com/videos**

By Amy Ellis Nutt / STAR-LEDGER STAFF

Ancient mariners believed the tides were the angry breathing of a sea creature chained to the ocean floor.

In Cape May on Sunday morning, Oct. 28, with Hurricane Sandy still 300 miles from shore, the tides, instead, beckon surfers, riding wind-driven swells off the Ocean Street beach.

Just inland, residents and business owners take the usual precautions against an impending storm. At the Congress Hall, where Abraham Lincoln once stayed, workers nail plywood over the ground-floor windows and doors.

Down Perry Street at the Bayberry Inn, a Victorian bed-and-breakfast, owners Andy and Toby Fontaine shuffle the patio furniture inside.

"We're staying, basically, because I can't think of any place to go," Andy Fontaine says.

The forecast has hovered like a Sword of Damocles over the state for days. Plenty of time to get ready — shore up windows, move possessions to second floors, purchase batteries and water. That's what New Jersey did last year, right before Irene hit. But this is different — a hurricane buddying with a nor'easter. Almost everyone believes the damage will be substantial and the pain, perhaps unprecedented. But few are prepared for the meteorological time bomb set to explode over New Jersey's coast, or the suddenness of a tidal surge that in the time it takes to watch a movie, will forever change the geography of the state.

While the Fontaines prepare for the storm, at Cape May Point Sister Mary Ann Mulzet moves briskly along the empty halls of St. Mary by-the-Sea, a massive Victorian structure built more than 120 years ago as a resort hotel. For the past 100 years, however, the Sisters of St. Joseph have called the 130-room hotel their retreat house. It stands sentinel on the southern-most piece of land in New Jersey — the last spit of earth where the toe of the Garden State meets the Atlantic.

SEE **SANDY,** PAGE 15

As lights turn on and transit resumes, New Jersey begins to move toward rebuilding — where it can

By Seth Augenstein and Mark Mueller
STAR-LEDGER STAFF

Trains are rolling again from Trenton to New York City. Nine out of 10 buses have resumed their routes. Hundreds of roads choked by debris have been

struck the region with the force of a thunderclap, crippling much of the state, New Jersey is showing the first stirrings of recovery.

Schools will open in a majority of districts tomorrow. Relief supplies and

to shake off the shock, he said. Now, he said, "It's time to forget about thinking backwards."

"We need to think forward," Christie said, "about how we return to normalcy."

Christie didn't sugarcoat the enormous

COMPLETE COVERAGE BEGINS ON PAGE 14

Utilities
As of 7 p.m., 1.2 million N.J. customers were without power. Page 16

FEMA
At least 49,000 Jerseyans

an even number may buy gasoline today. Page 17

The forecast
A slow-moving nor'easter seems increasingly likely to affect the state by

---

ABOVE: Rick Oliver of Berlin looks out at the water as his wife, Lynn, looks at a home destroyed by Hurricane Sandy on Saturday, Nov. 3. TONY KURDZUK/THE STAR-LEDGER

OPPOSITE: On some parts of the Shore, Hurricane Sandy left some homes so weakened that they collapsed, as happened to this beachfront property in Bay Head. TONY KURDZUK/THE STAR-LEDGER

BELOW: Manasquan beachfront residents are allowed back into their homes to gather belongings and view their property. PATTI SAPONE/THE STAR-LEDGER

ABOVE: National Guardsmen from McGuire Air Force Base stay warm at a checkpoint on Route 35 in Ortley Beach. NOAH K. MURRAY/THE STAR-LEDGER

ABOVE: Members of the New Jersey National Guard are pressed into service to distribute food, water and ice in Hazlet on Nov. 4. ED MURRAY/THE STAR-LEDGER

SUNDAY, NOV. 4 TO FRIDAY, NOV. 9

- "We're returning now to a new normal," Gov. Chris Christie declares.

- U.S. Homeland Security Secretary Janet Napolitano visits New Jersey and calls Hurricane Sandy "one of the largest natural disasters ever to hit the United States — a storm that covered an area the size of Western Europe."

- Federal Emergency Management Agency starts paying for temporary housing for people unable to be in their homes right away.

- To supplement suspended PATH trains and the flooded lower portion of the North Jersey Coast Line, the federal government provides 250 emergency buses to ferry commuters to Lower Manhattan.

- As the election arrives, New Jersey faces another major test in the wake of Sandy: maintaining the integrity of a presidential election in a storm-ravaged state. State and county officials scramble to ensure the election goes smoothly. Hundreds of damaged or blacked-out polling places have been moved. County clerks will be tested by an onslaught of paper ballots

- Sixty percent of the state's school districts remained closed, but many are expected to open soon. Superintendents cited outages, manpower shortages and damage to buildings.

TOP RIGHT: John Baldo prays before Sunday Mass in Holy Name Roman Catholic Church, which has been without power since the storm hit six days earlier in Union Beach. ED MURRAY/THE STAR-LEDGER

BOTTOM RIGHT: The lack of electricity did not prevent Father Mark Devlin from celebrating Mass at Holy Name in Union Beach on Sunday, Nov. 4. ED MURRAY/THE STAR-LEDGER

OPPOSITE: Lawrence DiGiorgio takes a moment to reflect during Sunday Mass at Holy Name. ED MURRAY/THE STAR-LEDGER

ABOVE: Utility crews brought in from out of state get to work along Route 206 near Peapack-Gladstone in Somerset County on Sunday, Nov. 4. Six days after the storm hit, many were still without power.

JERRY MCCREA/THE STAR-LEDGER

LEFT: Teesha Kubik of Long Valley splits wood from a century-old ash tree that fell on her grandparents' home in Schooley's Mountain in Morris County.

JERRY MCCREA/THE STAR-LEDGER

NOV. 4–NOV. 9 (CONT.)

- Hours-long lines for gasoline all but disappear as utility crews restore power to more service stations and more fuel flows into the state.
- All 12 casinos in Atlantic City are once more collecting cash. The last to open is the Atlantic Club Casino Hotel.
- Limited PATH service resumes.
- Route 35, the main thoroughfare in Ortley Beach, Seaside Heights and other communities, is now open to work crews through the southern part of Mantoloking.
- A nor'easter, just nine days after Hurricane Sandy hits the state, heaps fresh hardship and fear atop lingering misery.
- By the end of the week, an estimated 130,000 Jersey Central Power & Light customers and 57,000 Public Service Electric & Gas Co. customers were still without power.
- Christie said he would soon decide whether to rescind the odd-even gas-rationing plan he ordered.

RIGHT: Volunteers Renee Bracken, left, Jordan Smith, 10, and Eleanor Sappah, background, organize donated toiletries in a classroom at Keyport Central School in Monmouth County. Other rooms are dedicated to housing donations of food, clothing, bedding and even pet supplies. The school is being used as a shelter for 160 people.

ARISTIDE ECONOMOPOULOS/THE STAR-LEDGER

BOTTOM LEFT: People with gas cans and cars line up at a Delta gas station on McCarter Highway in Newark.

TIM FARRELL/THE STAR-LEDGER

BOTTOM RIGHT: Hundreds line up at Berkeley Township Municipal Building to get stickers that will allow them access to their houses on Monday, Nov. 5. Residents of South Seaside Park were allowed back onto the island to retrieve items, clean up and winterize their homes.

DAVID GARD/THE STAR-LEDGER

ABOVE: Volunteer Joy-Michele Tomczak, left, talks with shelter resident Dorothy Dole on Sunday, Nov. 4, at Keyport Central School. Dole, who is 101 years old, says this is the worst storm she has ever seen. ARISTIDE ECONOMOPOULOS/THE STAR-LEDGER

ABOVE: A woman walks on the beach in Bay Head, where sand has been piled up one week after Hurricane Sandy hit. JOHN MUNSON/THE STAR-LEDGER

LEFT: Ken Greulich gets rare use of a snow shovel at his summer home, as he removes sand from the yard of his house in the Midway Beach section of South Seaside Park. Residents were allowed back onto the island Monday, Nov. 5. DAVID GARD/THE STAR-LEDGER

BELOW: Debris litters the beach in Seaside Park looking toward Seaside Heights. The boardwalks and amusement areas in both were nearly obliterated by the storm. DAVID GARD/THE STAR-LEDGER

ABOVE: Toms River Assistant Fire Chief Eddie Storino, right, probationary firefighter Matthew Duell, center, and Safety Officer Philip Hann stop during a shift to vote at the Ocean County Administration Building in Toms River on Monday, Nov. 5. DAVID GARD/THE STAR-LEDGER

RIGHT: Voters wait their turn at the Ocean County Administration Building in Toms River on Monday, Nov 5, a day before the election. Early voting, extended mail balloting and lifted restrictions on polling locations were put in place to ease the process in affected areas.
DAVID GARD/THE STAR-LEDGER

ABOVE: Election worker Julio Castro of Jersey City sorts ballots that were dropped off by voters at the Hudson County Board of Elections in Jersey City on Monday, Nov. 5.

JOHN O'BOYLE/THE STAR-LEDGER

LEFT: On Election Day, voters in Bridgewater line up at a new polling place, the Bridgewater-Raritan High School, because the regular site was damaged in the storm. In affected areas across the state, polling places were moved or combined.

ED MURRAY/THE STAR-LEDGER

ABOVE: Aleksandar Kolarov walks through downed power lines — still not fixed on Monday, Nov. 5 — near his home on Highview Avenue in Bernardsville.

ED MURRAY/THE STAR-LEDGER

ABOVE: Rebecca Zdepski encounters a pile of wood and branches from her yard as she leaves her home in Bernardsville on Nov. 5. ED MURRAY/THE STAR-LEDGER

ABOVE: Workers close a breach in the barrier island at the base of the Mantoloking Bridge where Barnegat Bay met the Atlantic Ocean, on Monday, Nov. 5.

ANDREW MILLS/THE STAR-LEDGER

ABOVE: A long line of traffic slowly moves across the bridge and Pelican Island as residents of Seaside Park are allowed back onto the island on Monday, Nov. 5, to retrieve items, clean up and winterize their homes. DAVID GARD/THE STAR-LEDGER

LEFT: Power crews from Public Service Co. of Oklahoma replace a utility pole on Cedar Bridge Avenue in Brick on Tuesday, Nov. 6. ANDREW MILLS/THE STAR-LEDGER

ABOVE: A wheelchair is washed up on the beach in Bay Head. JOHN MUNSON/THE STAR-LEDGER

LEFT: Crews remove debris from destroyed homes in Bay Head on Monday, Nov. 5, one week after Hurricane Sandy hit.

JOHN MUNSON/THE STAR-LEDGER

ABOVE: The destroyed Joey Harrison's Surf Club remains in ruins on Monday, Nov. 5, in Ortley Beach. The owners have vowed to rebuild the well-known nightspot. ANDREW MILLS/THE STAR-LEDGER

LEFT: A message and a photo are left where a house once stood in Bay Head. JOHN MUNSON/THE STAR-LEDGER

FAR LEFT: Point Pleasant Beach residents continue to clean up and dig out on Monday, Nov. 5, one week after Hurricane Sandy struck. JOHN MUNSON/THE STAR-LEDGER

ABOVE: Jennifer Kulina-Lanse walks through a damaged area of Union Beach looking for stray cats left behind or abandoned or who have not found their way home. ARISTIDE ECONOMOPOULOS/THE STAR-LEDGER

RIGHT: Hetti Brown, center, and Jennifer Kulina-Lanse leave some cat food for strays in the area as Perry Stone, left, surveys the area with a Monmouth County detective on Tuesday, Nov. 6. Members of the Humane Society of the United States search for abandoned animals in a badly damaged area of Union Beach. ARISTIDE ECONOMOPOULOS/THE STAR-LEDGER

ABOVE: Perry Stone, right, looks into an unoccupied house, where numerous stray cats had reportedly moved in. Humane Society members continued their search for abandoned animals in Union Beach on Tuesday, Nov. 6. ARISTIDE ECONOMOPOULOS/THE STAR-LEDGER

ABOVE: Work crews stay busy cleaning up debris in Sea Bright on Thursday, Nov. 8.
NOAH K. MURRAY/THE STAR-LEDGER

OPPOSITE TOP: The cleanup on Ocean Avenue in Asbury Park leaves behind a mountain of sand on Tuesday, Nov. 6. NOAH K. MURRAY/THE STAR-LEDGER

OPPOSITE BOTTOM LEFT: Heavy equipment is brought in to attack the mound of damaged items left by residents and businesses along the Jersey Shore in Keansburg on Wednesday, Nov. 7. ROBERT SCIARRINO/THE STAR-LEDGER

OPPOSITE BOTTOM RIGHT: As a nor'easter hits the already devastated shore in Keansburg

on Wednesday, Nov. 7, Nick Hauser from Albert Marine Construction and James O'Neil from O'Neil Enterprises run drainage hoses over a newly built 15-foot sand berm from the pumps at the intersection of Beachway and Bayview Avenue in a effort to keep the area around Keansburg Beach from flooding again.
ROBERT SCIARRINO/THE STAR-LEDGER

ABOVE: Hoboken residents arriving to vote at the Boys & Girls Club on Tuesday, Nov. 6, find their polling place is closed due to damage from flooding. JENNIFER BROWN/THE STAR-LEDGER

LEFT: A Hoboken resident adds to the mountains of debris along the sidewalks of the once-heavily flooded areas of the city.
JENNIFER BROWN/THE STAR-LEDGER

BELOW: Employees of Farese Direct, contracted by the city of Hoboken, begin to pick up the piles of debris from the sidewalks.
JENNIFER BROWN/THE STAR-LEDGER

Barrier Island Districts from Toms River (#8 + #26), Berkeley Twp., Seaside Heights, Seaside Park & Lavallette - Vote at T.R. Hooper Avenue Elem. School - 1517 Hooper Avenue.

ABOVE: Toys and game cards are some of the Sandy casualties strewn about the damaged Keansburg Amusement Park on Tuesday, Nov. 6. ARISTIDE ECONOMOPOULOS/THE STAR-LEDGER

LEFT: The Hooper Avenue Elementary School polling place in Toms River was a busy one on Election Day as it became a destination for displaced voters from across Ocean County.
NOAH K. MURRAY/THE STAR-LEDGER

FAR LEFT: Leigh Busco and her son, Jake, leave Hooper Avenue Elementary School after she votes in Toms River.
NOAH K. MURRAY/THE STAR-LEDGER

ABOVE: The carousel at the Keansburg Amusement Park was crushed but not destroyed in the storm. The ride has been dismantled and the animals, even those that escaped in the flood, have been put in storage. ARISTIDE ECONOMOPOULOS/THE STAR-LEDGER

ABOVE: The Keansburg Amusement Park suffered extensive damage in Hurricane Sandy, but it was not the first time that the park had been devastated in a storm, and the owners plan to recover and reopen as they have done in the past. ARISTIDE ECONOMOPOULOS/THE STAR-LEDGER

ABOVE AND FAR LEFT: Workers at the Keansburg Amusement Park begin the task of cleaning up and rebuilding the heavily damaged attractions on Tuesday, Nov. 6. ARISTIDE ECONOMOPOULOS/THE STAR-LEDGER

LEFT: Brad Campoli adds to the pile of debris outside his home on Green View Drive in Toms River that was destroyed by Hurricane Sandy. NOAH K. MURRAY/THE STAR-LEDGER

ABOVE: A worker carries plywood sheathing to the top of the Great Auditorium in Ocean Grove as crews hurry to fabricate a new roof for the massive building on Tuesday, Nov. 6. ANDREW MILLS/THE STAR-LEDGER

RIGHT: From the exposed catwalk of the Great Auditorium in Ocean Grove, one can glimpse, 100 feet below, the damage to the historic theater. ANDREW MILLS/THE STAR-LEDGER

FAR RIGHT: Workers try to close up the gaping hole in the roof of the Great Auditorium in Ocean Grove on Monday, Nov. 5. The late-19th-century building has hosted entertainers from Tony Bennett to Bill Cosby to Ray Charles. ANDREW MILLS/THE STAR-LEDGER

ABOVE: Dave Simmer, left, and Matthew August, employees with the Keansburg Department of Public Works, set up a large pump at the intersection of Beachway and Bayview Avenue to prevent flooding from the nor'easter on Wednesday, Nov. 7. ROBERT SCIARRINO/THE STAR-LEDGER

LEFT: Gov. Chris Christie talks about preparation for an upcoming nor'easter, set to hit the state a little more than a week after Hurricane Sandy's devastating punch, on Wednesday, Nov. 7, at a news conference at the High Point Volunteer Fire Company in Harvey Cedars. NOAH K. MURRAY/THE STAR-LEDGER

ABOVE: The beach at Sandy Hook remains a mess on Thursday, Nov. 8. NOAH K. MURRAY/THE STAR-LEDGER

ABOVE: Manasquan Mayor George Dempsey, second from left, leads the borough council and other officials in the Pledge of Allegiance during a public meeting, held in a parking lot around an open fire because the municipal building was still without power on Thursday, Nov. 8. ANDREW MILLS/THE STAR-LEDGER

CHAPTER FIVE

Before and After Sandy

LEFT AND FAR LEFT:
The Thunderbird Hotel and smaller, bungalow-style ocean block homes just south in Brick Township as the Jersey Shore prepares for Hurricane Irene's arrival on Aug. 26, 2011 (far left). This area was destroyed by Hurricane Sandy 14 months later (left). ANDREW MILLS/ THE STAR-LEDGER

LEFT AND ABOVE: The Ocean Grove fishing pier in November 2009 (left) and the pier after Hurricane Sandy (above). ANDREW MILLS/THE STAR-LEDGER

ABOVE AND RIGHT: The Mantoloking Bridge as seen the morning after Tropical Storm Irene hit New Jersey on Aug. 29, 2011 (above). Devastation at the base of the Mantoloking Bridge where the Atlantic Ocean and Barnegat Bay created a new inlet after Hurricane Sandy destroyed areas of the Jersey Shore (right). ANDREW MILLS/THE STAR-LEDGER

ABOVE: The FunTown Pier in Seaside Park (left) and the Casino Pier in Seaside Heights the day after Tropical Storm Irene hit New Jersey in 2011.

ANDREW MILLS/THE STAR-LEDGER

RIGHT: The destroyed FunTown Pier in Seaside Park after Hurricane Sandy wreaked havoc on the Jersey Shore.

ANDREW MILLS/THE STAR-LEDGER

FAR RIGHT: Casino Pier in Seaside Heights after Hurricane Sandy struck.

ANDREW MILLS/THE STAR-LEDGER

CHAPTER SIX

Heroes

Sayreville, Population 42,704

Kindness — being a thing with powers to multiply — was headquartered in Sayreville, in a school cafeteria, compacted among piled rows of winter coats, blankets and shoes, baby formula, paper towels, about 200 boxes of rice, pasta and evaporated milk, easily more than 300 jars of canned vegetables and fruit, cat food and dog biscuits, and almost anything else a person somehow starting over would need.

At the back of the room at Our Lady of Victories Parish on Main Street stood Debbie DeMoor-Costantino, who is helping to lead a makeshift recovery team of neighbors and volunteers.

Like just about everyone else in Sayreville and surrounding Middlesex County towns, she and the others working with her first wore that dazed, untethered look, common across the state. In joining with one another, they have renewed old friendships and helped each other lift up from so much in Sayreville that has fallen down and been broken.

LEFT: Debbie DeMoor-Costantino, center (with blond hair and black shirt), poses with many of the volunteers manning the donation and relief center at Our Lady of Victories Parish in Sayreville, which was hit hard by Hurricane Sandy. Many credit DeMoor-Costantino as the primary organizer. TONY KURDZUK/THE STAR-LEDGER

Jennifer Kaufman, 47, Washington Township, Bergen County

The Teaneck High School teacher has had her Vespa for seven years.

Jennifer Kaufman pays only about $8 to fill the 2-gallon tank, which gets 70 to 80 miles per gallon. She's amassed 2,200 miles on the scooter, mostly cruising around local towns — when it's nice outside.

But after Hurricane Sandy, she jumped aboard the scooter, delivering supplies to Little Ferry and providing updates to the public on which gas stations were open.

ABOVE: Jennifer Kaufman of Washington Township pays only about $8 to fill the tank of her Vespa, which she used to deliver supplies and to alert people about gas station availability after Hurricane Sandy.
JOHN O'BOYLE/THE STAR-LEDGER

Gary Szatkowski, 55, Hainesport, Burlington County

The chief meteorologist at the local National Weather Service office in Mount Holly had his finger on his mouse — the panic button, essentially, for an entire region — ready to send an emergency briefing about a storm that didn't look like much of a threat in many ways.

It was a full six days before the newly named Hurricane Sandy touched ground in New Jersey. It was still 300 miles south of Jamaica. Most computer models had it moving harmlessly out to sea, and while a few had it curving into the New Jersey coast, no storm in modern history had ever done something like that.

The potential was too much to ignore. He issued some of the strongest warnings that anyone in the weather community had seen from a meteorologist in his position. He practically begged people to evacuate.

ABOVE: Gary Szatkowski, chief meteorologist at the National Weather Service office in Mount Holly, poses in the center's operations area. He is credited with providing an incredibly accurate forecast of Hurricane Sandy's strength and path that may have saved many lives.
TONY KURDZUK/THE STAR-LEDGER

Frank Smith Jr., 40, Little Ferry

You need only look at the front of Frank Smith Jr.'s house in Little Ferry to gather what his life has been like since Hurricane Sandy pummeled New Jersey.

On one side of the lawn are disheveled piles of waterlogged items: shoes, clothing, an end table, record albums, a hot water heater — all once stored in his basement, and all ruined by nearly 5 feet of water. On the other side are pallets of bottled water, bags filled with neatly packed towels and bed linens, clothing for adults and children. All donated for distribution to the families whose belongings were swept away in the floodwaters of Hurricane Sandy.

Smith is the volunteer captain of the Moonachie First Aid and Rescue Squad and assistant fire chief with the Moonachie Fire Department. He organizes some 80 volunteers in rescue and assistance operations, EMS and "fire rehab," giving first aid and assistance to working firefighters at fire scenes.

ABOVE: Frank Smith Jr., volunteer captain of the Moonachie First Aid and Rescue Squad, uses the front lawn of his water-damaged home in Little Ferry as a distribution center for goods donated to victims of Hurricane Sandy. JOHN O'BOYLE/THE STAR-LEDGER

Mavis Doozie, 36, Newark

There are many endeavors in which improvisation is highly prized, spontaneity encouraged, the rule book rewritten fearlessly on the fly. Obstetrics, generally speaking, is not one of them. Nor is traffic control.

Yet there was Mavis Doozie, 36 hours after Hurricane Sandy, in a traffic-choked intersection in southwest Newark. Fresh from delivering an 8-pound baby in the front seat of a station wagon, she madly ordered cars out of the way with her right arm, her left clutched around a mewling but healthy newborn, her clothes and shoes splattered bright red.

Doozie is a trained nurse, but until that day, she had never delivered a baby, much less on a city street with the eyes of an entire neighborhood upon her.

ABOVE: Charmanina Florence holds newborn baby Saed inside her Newark home as nurse Mavis Doozie and the baby's father, Qaadir Brooks, look on. Doozie helped deliver the baby after Hurricane Sandy hit. JOHN O'BOYLE/THE STAR-LEDGER

Katie Cataldo, 32, staff sergeant in the New Jersey National Guard, Vernon

The Hackensack River slipped from its banks. Those few residents of Moonachie and Little Ferry who managed to sleep through Hurricane Sandy awoke to a drowned world. The low-lying roads of these North Meadowlands towns had become canals, and the water, merciless and indifferent, invaded homes and swamped automobiles, leaving thousands stranded.

Even for a National Guard supply truck, it was a challenge. Staff Sgt. Katie Cataldo likes challenges.

With Staff Sgt. Brian Schooley beside her, the cheerful, sharp-eyed Cataldo led her team of 10 trucks and 20 soldiers into the flooded towns that Tuesday morning. They came at daybreak bearing bottled water and meals ready to eat. They left with trucks full of the old and infirm, mothers and children, and pets, taking those in need to safety and higher ground. Over three desperate days, the unit rescued 2,000 people.

LEFT: Katie Cataldo is a staff sergeant for the New Jersey National Guard who helped residents of Moonachie and Little Ferry after Hurricane Sandy hit the area. JOHN O'BOYLE/THE STAR-LEDGER

RIGHT: Russ "J" Gehweiler Jr. and Tracey Keelen pose against a snowy background during the post-Hurricane Sandy nor'easter. The lifeguards rescued people from Sandy's floodwaters after the storm hit. ED MURRAY/THE STAR-LEDGER

Russ "J" Gehweiler Jr., 30, and Tracey Keelen, 27, both of Toms River

The Tuesday morning after the hurricane, the two lifeguards packed their wetsuits and towels into a Jeep and drove to Brick to Russ "J" Gehweiler's father's house. The couple soon realized they were about to enter a scene unlike anything they had ever witnessed. The water was waist deep. They began to walk. When "J" came upon a stray surfboard, he grabbed it and began to paddle. On his way toward his father's house, neighbors shouted to him.

"I'll come back for you," J shouted. "After I get to my dad."

Near his father's house, J saw the bow of a boat underwater. He paddled over, pulled out the knife he'd packed, and began to cut the rope that held the boat to the trailer. It sprang to the surface like a cork.

Keelen had stayed behind with the Jeep at first, but after an hour of shuttling people to safety, she joined J on the boat to rescue about four dozen people.

Loucious Jones, 45, Newark

He doesn't rely on his cane with the red tip to get around Newark. He banks on the little vision in his left eye, because he can't see a thing in the right.

Loucious Jones is legally blind, but it's not a problem when he ambles down the street, going door to door in Newark. At each home he approaches, the message is simple for whoever answers or sticks their head out the window in his neighborhood. He tells them where they can go for food and supplies because he knows they're hurting from Hurricane Sandy.

In the aftermath of this storm, Jones has been a foot soldier on the ground. His wife of 26 years, Sabrina, and their three daughters have been in the streets with him, too.

Chuck Beverly, 52, Atlantic City; Frank Bright, Atlantic City; Francisco Ortiz, 47, Atlantic City; Howard Search, 56, Atlantic City

They're four guys, street-wise, from Atlantic City.

A former crack user with piercing eyes and a camo hoodie. A short, stocky cook who once worked at Tropicana and Caesars. A Harley-tattooed construction worker, who recently completed a five-month stretch in jail. And the most flamboyant of the four, a former men's clothing salesman who happens to be a church elder and owner of a dog named Pookie.

Four guys named Frank, Chuck, Howard and Francisco.

These four men — call them the 4 Live Kitchen Crew, or Men with (an Odd Collection of) Hats — didn't do anything dramatic during Hurricane Sandy. They didn't pull a drowning child out of a swollen creek or pluck a grandmother off a roof. They just showed up for work and did their job: Feed the hungry.

Jeannette Van Houten, 42, Union Beach

She is rescuing the memories of Union Beach, one muddied 5-by-7 snapshot or soaked wedding album at a time.

Photographs have ended up blocks from the living rooms where they were lovingly displayed. They are scattered in backyards and gutters, in reedy marshes and beaches, and all along the narrow, debris-strewn streets. For many people, these images are all that remain of life as it was before Sandy.

Jeannette Van Houten has spent hours scanning hundreds of the orphaned photos so they could be uploaded to Facebook. Her goal was to establish a Sandy-related online lost-and-found for the precious images of loved ones. Within a week after Sandy's punch, more than 500 photographs had been posted on the page, titled "Union Beach — Photos and misplaced items."

RIGHT: Jeannette Van Houten, 42, hopes to return all the photos that she found scattered in Union Beach to their owners. "It's a little piece of their past, something they can hold on to," she says. "FEMA can't take it away, the building inspector can't. ... Mother Nature can try, but it can come back to us."

PATTI SAPONE/THE STAR-LEDGER

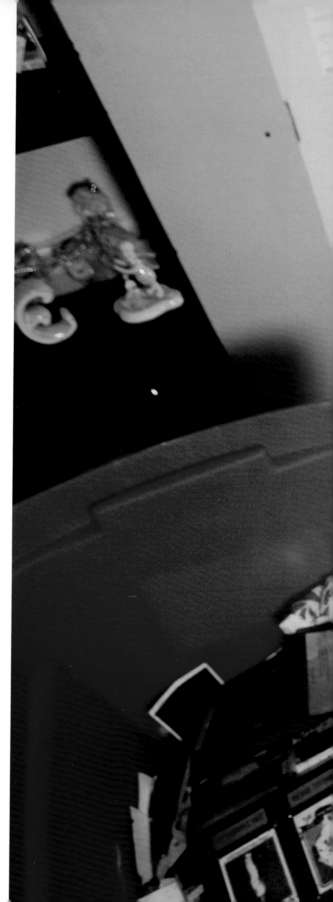

Jay Price, 42, Manasquan

As he inched through the churning, chest-deep water, Jay Price struggled to distinguish one potential catastrophe from the next. Fifty-foot oak trees snapped in violent crackles like broomsticks all around him. The 60 mph winds howled like a freight train speeding down the tracks. Broken telephone poles torpedoed over the top of the flooding waters.

Price and his comrades from Manasquan Hook and Ladder Company No. 1 kept pushing forward on that late Oct. 29 night. The group navigated the rushing water, the debris and the danger to reach stranded people in their homes and rescue them to the safety of their M35 Army cargo truck, through

most of the chaotic night.

The next day, he went house to house searching the rubble for gas leaks. The Manasquan High School varsity football coach also enlisted his 94 football players as volunteer workers in town.

Robert Felberg, 44, Morristown

It's the Friday after Sandy, and neurologist Robert Felberg is stuck in his Morristown home without power. Downed trees and power lines litter the roads and trap him in his neighborhood. In Teaneck, an elderly man who has just suffered a stroke has been admitted to Holy Name Hospital.

Every minute the elderly man goes without treatment, 2 million brain cells die. Immediate help makes the difference between returning to normal life and being permanently impaired.

Felberg grabs his computer and hops into his green Toyota Tundra pickup truck in search of a 4G signal. Twenty-five minutes later, he finds service. Working with a team leader, he's able to see a clot blocking blood flow to nearly a third of the brain. He's then able to prescribe a treatment. The blood clot dissolves and the patient later is able to go home.

ABOVE: Robert Felberg, director of the Comprehensive Stroke Center at Overlook Medical Center, oversaw the treatment of a stroke patient from a laptop in his truck. Felberg's home in Morristown was without power and he could not get to the patient, at Holy Name Hospital. JENNIFER BROWN/THE STAR-LEDGER

Bill MacDonald, 62, Bridgewater

He has done business in town since 1977, when it was mostly farmland, and Bill MacDonald can point out when and where each development sprang up on the green hills and Watchung ridges that look down on his hardware store at the epicenter of Warren Township.

When Hurricane Sandy snapped the lights out in Warren at 8 p.m. Oct. 29, it roiled a corner of Bill MacDonald's heart and triggered a series of bold business maneuvers they don't teach you at Wharton.

He sent workers in trucks to as far away as New Hampshire to pick up supplies, and with residents having no access to power or money because the ATMs weren't working in northern Somerset County, he allowed people in town to purchase on faith.

ABOVE: Bill MacDonald, owner of Warrenville Paint and Hardware, and employee Richard Seale work at the epicenter of Warren Township. MacDonald let people purchase on faith after the storm. JOHN O'BOYLE/THE STAR-LEDGER

OPPOSITE: Jay Price kneels in front of rescue team members, from left, Mike Samuel, Sean Price, Patrick Kesler, Paul Samuel, Ryan Dullea and Kevin Richey. Price led a team of firefighters on water rescues as Hurricane Sandy slammed into the Jersey Shore, flooding 60 percent of Manasquan. The Manasquan High School varsity football coach also enlisted 94 football players as volunteers in town. ANDREW MILLS/THE STAR-LEDGER

CHAPTER SEVEN

Lives Lost

by Jessica Calefati, Seth Augenstein, Victoria St. Martin and Bob Braun

Hurricane Sandy took the lives of 39 New Jersey residents. The youngest was 4 years old and the oldest was 94. Some died on the night Sandy hit, but most died long after the hurricane left New Jersey. Many were struck by falling tree limbs. And some died in their cold homes either of hypothermia or from accidental falls in the dark.

ROBERT PATTERSON

Robert and Karyl Patterson stayed active in their retirement and they stayed happy together into their 47th year of marriage. Robert Patterson, 79, decided to stay home alone at their Lambertville house during the post-Hurricane Sandy nights without electricity. His wife stayed with family members who had power. She came back to pick him up on Election Day to go to the polls together. But when she entered their house, Karyl Patterson found her husband lying on the floor. He was declared dead by EMTs. The state medical examiner ruled he died from a fall the day before, Nov. 5.

LEONARD THOMPSON

Leonard Thompson was known on his street as a neighborly but private man. He spent much time tinkering with his two cars up on jacks, friends recall. After Hurricane Sandy he was found dead in his cold and flooded Stafford Township home. Neighbors who had evacuated the neighborhood returned to find his two cars still in the driveway, crushed by a fallen tree.

Thompson, 71, who suffered from a heart condition, died of hypothermia, according to the state medical examiner.

ROBERT MAYBERRY

Robert Mayberry loved the ocean. Sailing, boating, fishing and surfing. It all came naturally.

His Long Branch apartment was a block from the beach, and he'd point his specially made beach-cruiser bicycle to the sand whenever he could. The 61-year-old man died of hypothermia in his unheated apartment.

THOMAS FREY

Thomas Frey enjoyed hiking with friends from Pattenburg, his tiny hometown in Hunterdon County. His friends said he was a naturalist with an artist's eye who used his camera to capture the beauty of his rural community.

Frey ran the Pattenburg General Store and lived in town with his father. The 44-year-old man died Oct. 31 while using a chainsaw to break down felled trees and limbs from Pattenburg's streets. He suffered severe head trauma after being struck with a tree limb.

WILLIAM HARDENBURG

William Hardenburg wore his brown cowboy boots everywhere. The 67-year-old wore them to work as Bethlehem Township's Office of Emergency Management coordinator. He wore them to services at Phillipsburg Alliance Church, where he served as head deacon.

William Hardenburg died Nov. 5 after being struck by a pickup truck while helping clear Hurricane Sandy debris from a Raritan Township roadway. The married father of two and stepfather of three was one of two Pattenburg first responders to die from storm-related injuries.

JOSEPH GODLESKI

Joseph Godleski's herniated disc forced him to walk with a cane, but the retiree's injury didn't stop him from a tradition he began shortly after retiring from his work in sales at an Englewood fastener company. Each morning he visited a Dunkin Donuts, located less than one mile from his South Hackensack home, and returned with two extra large decaffeinated coffees prepared with extra milk.

When he awoke around 5:30 a.m. on Oct. 30, the day after rain from Sandy flooded the nearby Hackensack River, Godleski persisted in his routine. His wife, Barbara, was still asleep. The 69-year-old never came home. His body and his 2002 Mazda were recovered in floodwater near the Dunkin Donuts. His cane was inside the vehicle.

JOSEPH PUGLISI

Joseph Puglisi met his wife, Alice, down the Shore at a dance hall in Asbury Park. He followed Alice's pretty Irish girlfriends, the Jennings sisters, into the club, and they led him straight to her, she said. The inseparable pair were married 62 years. Puglisi, 93, died when he fell down a flight of stairs in their darkened Summit home Oct. 31.

LESTER KAPLAN

The water had never come up to their house on Lafayette Boulevard in Brigantine, Lester Kaplan told his wife, Atara. There was just no reason to worry, despite the mandatory evacuation order issued.

So Kaplan stayed behind, said his wife. Lester Kaplan, 73, was a retired lawyer who was an avid swimmer. He also liked to frequent the nearby casinos. But he had a heart problem. And on Nov. 2, after the storm had passed, he succumbed to hypothermia. Emergency responders found Kaplan unresponsive in his cold and dark home. He died on the way to the hospital.

BRUCE LATTERI

Bruce Latteri was at a friend's house watching and listening to Hurricane Sandy's approach late on the night of Oct. 29, when a tree slammed its front porch only feet away from where he was sitting, just missing him.

Latteri decided to walk back to his own house on the same street, Nicole Court, in the Cozy Lake section of Oak Ridge. He told his friend he was worried about his dog. But early Tuesday morning, as the 51-year-old Latteri sat at his kitchen table, another tree crashed through the roof of his home, striking his head and killing him instantly.

ERWIN BOCKHORN

The night Hurricane Sandy hit, Erwin Bockhorn's daughter told him to go up to the attic of his home in Little Egg Harbor Township and stay there just in case the downstairs was flooded. He told his daughter not to worry — in previous storms, the water had never come through the front door.

Sometime early on Tuesday, the deluge came. The water swept into Bockhorn's house. The water crested above the kitchen counter. He was found by a neighbor. Authorities ruled he had drowned — but the medical experts aren't sure whether he was asleep at the time the water rushed in, or whether the 72-year-old, who suffered from Parkinson's disease, just couldn't get up the stairs and was caught in the flood.

EVA-MARIA WILSON

Eva-Maria Wilson survived World War II as a child in Germany. She escaped the firebombing of Dresden, her hometown, when more than 100,000 died in one night. She nearly starved after the war ended. Then, nearly 80, she even endured the worst of Hurricane Sandy — only to die in a fall down the stairs of her dark Berkeley Heights home more than a week after the storm passed.

WILLIAM SWORD Jr.

After a deranged student nearly killed him with a knife at his Princeton home nine years ago, William Sword Jr. "reset" his life, according to a family member. Enjoying each day and spending time with family — his wife, Martha, their three children — became even more central to the life of the busy financier.

During the peak of the storm, the 61-year-old managing director of Wm. Sword & Co. was clearing the driveway outside his Princeton home when a tree fell on him and killed him almost instantly.

GEORGE TATAY

George Tatay was raised in the Hungarian city of Gyor on the River Danube, halfway between Vienna and Budapest. Each spring, the river spilled over its banks, and he and his brother, Carl, were terrified of the power of the water.

The family escaped Hungary for Austria and ultimately came to the United States. George wound up in coastal Brick. George Tatay, 61, drowned in his Vanard Drive home, in several feet of water, on Oct. 30, during the height of the storm. The state Attorney General's Office reported heart disease contributed to his death.

MAUREEN CAPORINO

Maureen Caporino's philosophy about greeting visitors to the Jersey City Municipal Utilities Authority was simple: Strangers must be vetted. Caporino, 65, would tilt her head, raise one eyebrow and grill visitors she didn't recognize with questions about their credentials. Caporino worked at the authority for 22 years before retiring with severe health problems. Chronic obstructive pulmonary disease made it difficult for Caporino to breathe.

She was found dead by her caretaker in her modest two-story home on Ogden Avenue in Jersey City on Oct. 30 less than 24 hours after the power went out. The oxygen tanks on which she relied could not operate; emergency tanks that relied on batteries were empty.

MARY LOU VISWAT

They wished each other good night and, while the winds of Sandy howled around them, each added something. Mary Lou Viswat and her only child, Henry Viswat, told each other, "I love you."

The next day, Henry found his 84-year-old mother at the bottom of her basement stairs. She had fallen to her death in the darkness. Mary Lou Viswat had been an active woman. She retired after a career as a teacher at Bound Brook High School where she also served as head of the business department. She also was a borough councilwoman and was active in community organizations.

VERNIE MATHISON

When Hurricane Sandy hit on Oct. 29, Vernie Mathison's West Orange home lost power for only three minutes, but the brief electrical failure was enough to kill him.

In 2009, Mathison was diagnosed with amyotrophic lateral sclerosis, commonly known as Lou Gehrig's disease. The degenerative, fatal condition attacks brain and spinal cord cells that control voluntary muscle movement. Mathison, 61, had slowly deteriorated since his diagnosis and was bedridden when the hurricane struck. The oxygen machine he relied on to help him breathe failed when his home lost power. He died nine days later on Nov. 7 due to complications from respiratory and heart failure.

RICHARD AND ELIZABETH EVERETT

The love between Rich and Beth Everett was often on display in the kitchen of their Randolph home. A smile while washing dishes, a hug after breakfast, a kiss on the cheek before bed. Rich, 54, worked as a chemist, but often, he dressed like a cowboy. Rich and Beth, 48, owned a horse farm, and in recent years, he had taken up a style of Western riding known as reining. The new hobby influenced his wardrobe.

The couple were returning to their home in Randolph from their horse farm, the Blue Crest Riding Center in Long Valley, on Oct. 29 when a 100-foot-tall, 3-foot-wide tree toppled by hurricane-force winds fell on the cab of their pickup truck, killing the couple.

FLETCHER FISH

Fletcher Fish had a good soul, said a friend. It was obvious in his love of art, his endowment of a scholarship for aspiring musicians, his concern for his friends. On the night Hurricane Sandy slammed in New Jersey, Henry Ingrassia, a friend, said Fish called to check on him. An hour later, Fish, 77, who served as chairman of the William Paterson University Foundation, was killed when two trees crashed through the roof and into the second floor bedroom of his home on Kingston Avenue in Hawthorne.

BOBBY McDUFFIE

Bobby McDuffie knew a storm was coming, but he also knew he had the chance to work an extra shift and bring home more money for his family. He went to work at a food warehouse on Euclid Avenue in Newark Oct. 29 and he never came home.

Newark Police Director Samuel DeMaio said workers at the warehouse could see the Passaic River flooding and water was rushing down Joseph Street near the warehouse. McDuffie and other employees took a break to move their cars. He never came back to work. The next day, McDuffie, 47, was found drowned in his car.

KENYA BARBER AND MUDIWA BENSON

Kenya Barber and Mudiwa Benson were cousins and best friends, young women so close they were often mistaken for sisters. The women, who graduated together from Newark's Malcolm X Shabazz High School, were friendly and outgoing.

The women sought each other out during the storm. Benson, 18, whose home had no power, moved in with Barber, 19, at Riverside Court in Newark. Barber had a generator that she had installed on the outside of her home.

But something went wrong. Police say the generator was placed under an open window and the difference in temperatures created a vacuum that sucked carbon monoxide fumes into the room where they slept. Their bodies were found on the evening of Oct. 31.

ROBERT WALSH

Robert Walsh spent 25 years with the Edison Fire Department before he retired a decade ago. He had spent three hours waiting in line for a generator before the storm. When the storm came, it knocked out power.

Police say a friend became concerned about Walsh about 36 hours after someone else had spoken to him and the friend broke into his single-family home off Woodbridge Avenue. They found the generator in the garage, nearly out of fuel. They found Walsh on his couch, unresponsive. Authorities say he died of carbon monoxide poisoning.

CHARLENE AND EDWIN JORDAN

Charlene and Edwin Jordan were found dead inside their Willingboro home after a blaze swept through the house. Officials said the Jordans were using a gas generator because they lost power during the storm, but the blaze apparently was caused by an electrical problem.

Edwin Jordan, 74, had been an aircraft mechanic with the Air Force. His wife, Charlene, 70, was a nurse forced into retirement after she was disabled in an accident. She had not been able to walk for two years. They met five decades ago in Elyria, Ohio, but traveled the world together because of his military postings.

MARGARET PRIDDY AND LAWRENCE E. PRIDDY JR.

Margaret and Lawrence Priddy were fixtures each Sunday at the Middlesex Presbyterian Church. The mother and son sat in the third row and were familiar to other congregants because she was a deacon who sang in the choir. But they were not there the first Sunday after Hurricane Sandy struck.

Early the previous day, Margaret and her 57-year-old son were trapped in a fire that ravaged their home just a mile away from the church. Emergency service workers pulled the 78-year-old woman out of the single-story house. They found her by the front door, but she died 10 days later. Her son was found in the basement, dead of smoke inhalation. Another relative, not identified by police, escaped the blaze. Police attribute the fire to the candles the family used for light after their home lost power.

GRACIE DUNSTON

It was tragedy enough when Gracie Dunston died during the storm, but it could have been a lot worse. She succumbed to carbon monoxide poisoning in her Trenton home but, when emergency workers arrived, they found seven other family members suffering from near asphyxiation.

James Minus, Gracie's husband for more than 40 years, said their youngest son found her unresponsive in a bedroom less than an hour after she disappeared from the family the night of Oct. 31.

Life was hard for Gracie Dunston — the 59-year-old worked at a Cranbury farm, cleaning spinach — but she spent what time she could making life easier for her husband and her large family. That included bringing as many as she could back to her modest home during the storm where she could feed and look after them.

VERNON HANKINS

After the storm passed, Vernon Hankins told some colleagues at Brick Township High School he felt lucky he weathered the storm so well. Sure, his house on Nejecho Drive flooded and was all but destroyed. Still, if the tree in his yard had fallen on the house, it would have been much worse.

A few days after that conversation, on the morning of Thanksgiving, Hankins, 61, was killed by that same tree. It had been uprooted during the worst of the storm, leaving a large hole behind. Hankins climbed into the hole to cut at the tree's roots so he could remove the stump. The tree shifted and fell on him. He died not long after he was taken to Ocean Medical Center.

BERNICE SAPP

Bernice Sapp was a born helper. She worked for years as a nurse at the King David Care Center nursing home, but also volunteered at numerous churches and soup kitchens in the Atlantic City area, including Sister Jean's Kitchen.

But Sapp's career and good works quickly came to an end with a stroke in recent years, and the 65-year-old woman lived off Social Security — part of the reason she moved to the Altman Terrace public apartments. She died during the evacuation of the apartments. The Attorney General's Office has concluded that it was storm-related.

CELESTINE KREITZER

Celestine Kreitzer survived much in her life. She outlived two husbands. She endured storms before in her Forked River home. When Hurricane Sandy bore down on Ocean County, she refused to leave her home. But this storm was something Kreitzer hadn't experienced in her 94 years. And, on Oct. 30, during the height of the wind and the rain and the darkness and the cold, she died alone from hypothermia while several feet of water swirled in her Oakwood Drive house, according to the Ocean County Prosecutor's Office.

ALICE REDZILOW

Alice Redzilow lived her entire life in Bayonne, a small, working-class city located south of Jersey City in Hudson County. She was born there at Bayonne Medical Center in 1926 and died in her Linden Avenue home at age 86. When Hurricane Sandy began pummeling the city where she was raised, Redzilow decided to ride out the storm in her home despite mandatory orders to evacuate. While using the bathroom in her darkened home, Redzilow slipped and struck her head, possibly on the bathroom's doorknob, officials said. She died from loss of blood caused by the injury and was discovered five days after the storm struck.

DHYANESH BALAJI

Dhyanesh Balaji owned a small red bicycle with black handles and black training wheels. Neighbors occasionally saw the 4-year-old riding the sleek bike up and down Laidlaw Avenue in Jersey City, where he lived in a second-floor apartment with his mother and grandmother. At 6:30 p.m. on Halloween, a car driven by a neighbor struck the child while he was crossing a darkened street with his mother and grandmother. The intersection of Jefferson Avenue and Central Avenue was one of thousands throughout Jersey City that was dark that night. Nearly the entire city of 250,000 was without power two days after Hurricane Sandy struck.

RAFAEL REYES

When Rafael Reyes left the Dominican Republic nearly 20 years ago, his wife waited for him to return and bring her to the United States. Tomasina Almonte Reyes joined her husband in New Brunswick where they raised three children and opened a restaurant.

Two days after Hurricane Sandy struck, Reyes left his New Brunswick home. The 52-year-old man never returned. His body was found a day later in the kitchen of their restaurant, La Sajoma, located just a few blocks from their home. He died of carbon monoxide poisoning. The new generator he had purchased was found in the basement of the restaurant.

WILLIAM PRYOR

Bill Pryor was an unlikely yet essential member of the crisis response team at Robert Wood Johnson University Hospital in Hamilton. He was a pharmacist. Pryor, 58, drove through darkened streets and pelting rain to make it on time for his regularly scheduled overnight shift in Hamilton on Oct. 29, the day Hurricane Sandy struck. He had just parked his car and was walking through the hospital's parking lot when a strong gust of hurricane-force wind blew the large man off his feet, twice.

He sustained a blunt force trauma injury to his torso and died due to complications from the fall 12 days later on Nov. 10.

WALTER SCHOEPFER

By Oct. 30, much of the storm's violence had subsided in the southernmost areas of New Jersey, but the surging waters on the bay side of Ventnor City were still at their peak. That's when Walter Schoepfer, 93, a World War II veteran, decided to try to move his car away on North Oxford Street.

He found himself in swirling waters more than 4 feet deep. He fell and struck his head, according to the state medical examiner. He lived for another week but died Nov. 6.

AMADEO GUTIERREZ

On Nov. 6, Amadeo Gutierrez, a landscaper, had been called to remove a partially damaged tree on Tutor Place in East Brunswick, some eight miles from his North Brunswick home. While up in the tree trying to clear away limbs, one large section of the tree suddenly shifted, striking the 41-year-old man and killing him.

ERNEST WILLIAMS

Ernest Williams, 65, loved to play with the children in his extended family, extending his arms and letting them climb the branches of his strong arms. The retired steelworker also would privately help friends and relatives who needed it.

But he also suffered from asthma and, when Hurricane Sandy struck and the power in his Newark senior housing building went out, Ernest Williams was in peril. He was found Nov. 4 with an empty inhaler in his hand. His death, according to the state medical examiner, was due to an acute asthma excaberbation.

BERNICE PASQUARELLO

Nearly a month after Hurricane Sandy decimated shore towns like Sea Isle City, it claimed a 39th victim.

Bernice Pasquarello returned to Sea Isle City the weekend after Thanksgiving to inspect her home and survey the town's damage. A team of Sea Isle City Department of Public Works employees were gathering debris off the town's roadways.

While walking along a main road that was recently reopened, Bernice Pasquarello saw the small dump truck coming toward her and "stepped out" of its way. Pasquarello did not notice when the dump truck stopped and began to drive in reverse. The driver did not see her either and accidentally hit the 69-year-old woman while backing up.

Credits

Editors:
Steve Liebman, Seth Siditsky

Writers:
Seth Augenstein, Jeff Bradley, Bob Braun, Jessica Calefati, Barry Carter, Tomás Dinges, Peter Genovese, Vicki Hyman, Victoria St. Martin, Tris McCall, Amy Ellis Nutt, Linda Ocasio, Steve Politi, Ronni Reich, Matthew Stanmyre, Stephen Stirling, Craig Wolff

Photographers:
Jennifer Brown, Tomás Dinges, Aristide Economopoulos, Tim Farrell, Chris Faytok, David Gard, Saed Hindash, Tony Kurdzuk, Tim Larsen, Jerry McCrea, Frances Micklow, Andrew Mills, John Munson, Ed Murray, Noah K. Murray, John O'Boyle, William Perlman, Patti Sapone, Robert Sciarrino

Graphics:
Andre Malok

Copy Editors:
Patricia K. Cole, Brittney Davies, Mark DiMartini, Kelly Duncan, Joe Green, Jennifer Potash, Craig Schmidt, Frank Verde

Design and Production:
Chris Fenison and Brandon Kays, Pediment Publishing

Marketing:
Doug Hutton, Robert Provost